God

Strength

Build a Strong Mind, a Strong Spirit, and a Strong Body.

Stephanie A. Wright

This book is dedicated to my mother, Valerie.

My mother, due to multiple life traumas of her own, had many flawed thinking patterns and coping mechanisms that did not serve her and inhibited her from being who she was created to be for much of her life. However, my mother possesses an amazing spirit that does not give up; battered, beaten, and abused she has always continued to get back up. Her life is a testimony of God's saving and redeeming power. She has often shared her testimony, including her short-comings, while teaching and peaching the word of God over the past 11 years. It takes a strong, determined spirit, and a set mind to begin to change thinking patterns, and to overcome shame and/or depression —she does this, and openly shares her story to effect change in others. I am grateful to receive her support in this book and am very proud of who she is. She is smart, faithful, resilient and loving. It's my hope that this book will encourage her, and others, to continue to strengthen their minds, spirits, and bodies.

Acknowledgements

I'm grateful to God for the people He has placed in my life to encourage me to completion of this book. Although I am not able to thank every person who has offered support and prayers, I must thank Jeanette for pushing me to accept the ministry calling God has placed on me, Robyn for challenging and encouraging me when I didn't believe that I could complete my assignment, and Katie, my editor and friend, for helping me express my thoughts and knowledge so practically. I love and am grateful for each of you.

To my husband, my confidant, and my covering – your unwavering love, support, and patience through this process has been one of my greatest blessings. Thank you for loving me as Christ loved the church; I pray I reflect that same love back to you. You make my heart smile.

Not only did you cover me with love when I was exhausted, distracted, or emotional, but you and Malachi spent countless hours staying quiet and out for the main rooms so I could write in solitude. Thank you both; our family is the most precious gift to me and I sincerely hope the ministry of this book will be worth your sacrifice over the last several months. I love you both beyond words.

Lastly, and most importantly, I must give all praise to God for His incomprehensible love for me. Thank you for being the same loving, merciful, and gracious God that gave the perfect sacrifice, that saved my life and reminds me daily that I'm worthy. I am in awe that you would use me, and I pray that your love and work be manifested through me, that my life would bring you glory.

Note to the Reader

Dear Reader,

Thank you for picking up this book, it is my sincere prayer that this book will move you closer to God and help you to develop a strong and sound mind, a strong spirit, and a strong body. My personal pains and promises, my failures and my faith, laid the foundation for this book. Within the introduction to this book you will find a small part of the personal testimony that has helped shape who I am and what I've learned on my personal journey. Although I've shared minimal detail and only a few stories, if you have suffered abuse, the introduction may be a trigger for you. If stories of abuse are triggering for you, please be mindful before moving on to the introduction(or feel free to skip right over it). The book is written so that if you need to skip the introduction, you will still be able to follow the subsequent text and get all the information you need to begin building your strong mind, strong spirit, and strong body.

Yours in Christ,

Stephanie A. Wright

Table of Contents

Part Three – Building a Strong Body

Introduction

In the fall of 2005, I found myself sitting in the middle of my bathroom floor holding a bottle of pills and contemplating a way out. I was married and had extended family, yet I felt entirely alone, and I had given in to depression. As I sat there, I searched myself for a reason to live, for some worth in my life. Finding none, I desperately called to God sure He would not answer, but He did. He answered in such a way that I will never forget it. The undeniable presence of God opened my eyes and saved my life.

When I got up from that floor and looked in the mirror the reflection was not one of someone who had peace, joy, or victory. The reflection was one of a child. The truth was that I was stuck —stuck in my pain and stuck in a flawed pattern of thinking. One of my earliest memories was one that made me sick to contemplate; it was the memory of an event that would, seemingly, set the tone for much of my childhood...

My mom had a habit of dating the wrong men – always. One man, a recovering alcoholic, dated my mom for several months. During that time he befriended me – or so I thought. He let me taste his non-alcoholic beer(I'm not sure that's even a thing, but I remember the green bottle, and the taste). He shared funny stories with me, and then he began sharing more. One day, while I was playing Barbies in my room, he came in and dropped his pants. He asked me to kiss his penis. I was absolutely horrified; not because I understood what was happening, but because as I explained to him "that's where my brothers pee from and I don't want pee in my mouth". He quickly left, leaving me confused and sad that I had made him unhappy while he was always so kind to me. Several days later, when he asked me to sit on his lap while my mother was cooking dinner in the next room, I happily obliged thinking the other day was forgotten. I was wrong. He whispered how I had hurt his feelings, and then proceeded to move around my shorts so he could stick his finger in me... FEAR — this was the moment when fear first entered my life.

To say that my brothers and I had a difficult upbringing would be an understatement. The fact is that we were exposed to too much. Children should not be exposed to guns and drugs, much less be expected to hide them. Children should not be subject to an ever-changing array of people or, without thought, be left unattended. This, however, was our reality. Fear continued to be a big part of our lives as we grew older. In fact, you could say that life gave way to fear...

After spending the better part of a year at our grandparents my brothers and I were thrilled to be back with our mom, but the day that we moved back from our grandparents we found that she was shacked up with a guy whom we will call "Kevin". He had a background in martial arts. Kevin was very authoritative and, like many of the men that would follow, he seemed to have a spilt personality at first. However, the longer he stayed, the less spilt his personality became and the more abusive it was towards us kids. With my mother he behaved lovingly, to the point of my disgust. My brothers and I, however, increasingly became objects on which aggression and frustration were taken out. School was escape for us. We made up homework to seem busy. We lived in fear daily. Beatings started to become daily occurrences.

Threats to our safety seemed to come hourly. No offense was too small to warrant a beating, and when mom arrived home from work, she made no protest. That was probably the most heartbreaking piece. She did not, and as an adult I realize that she could not, protect us. As the number and frequency of beatings increased, so did the modes and intensity. No one knew what we suffered — not even our closest friends. Fear and pain became what we expected and what we survived daily. We were good at hiding bruises. We were good at hiding pain. We accepted it as what our life would be. Until one day my youngest brother was beaten with a wrestling belt until he passed out, and was, consequently, so severely welted that it could not be hidden. Why, you ask? He was beaten for asking me for a piece of paper for his homework. My little brother was told that he should have told Kevin that he needed more paper; that (simply asking for school supplies) was apparently what warranted the worst beating that my younger brother ever received. My older brother and I were so scared that our brother would be beaten to death that we finally told our mom that if she didn't get rid of him, we would call the police. Despite all the physical and

13

sexual abuse I had up to that point endured, and would later endure, the memory of this day will always remain the most traumatic. The vision of my little brother that day will be forever present.

Immediately following this event, my mother announced that she would not date again until all us kids were out of the house. After watching us children being severely abused for much of our lives, my mother realized she was not making great choices, and she promised would wait until we were gone before she had another boyfriend. Turns out she waited about three months. The next man she decided to date (we'll call him Eugene) was 10 years my senior and 12 years her junior...

I happened to be good friends with Eugene's sister and he was giving us a ride one day; that's how my mother met him. They began dating and things seemed to go along well enough for about a year, and then they got married. It was also about this time that Eugene got our family involved in church, and we started going to a Baptist Church. I was somewhat engaged in church, and although I wasn't fully sold out for Christ, I enjoyed going. Shortly after their marriage (Summer 1997/1996) Eugene started harassing me sexually. Somewhere in the mix of all of this I started feeling very uncomfortable, and I understood that my pastor was supposed to look out for me, so I went to see him. Instead of helping me, my pastor was convinced that I was part of the problem because I looked a certain way and because my mother's husband had convinced him that I was a fast girl. At the time, I was still a virgin, but I understood even at the age of 14 that Eugene wanted to have sex with me and would likely rape me to get it. Given all the abuse that I had faced earlier in life and all of the times that my mother had looked away, I believed in my heart that it was inevitable. So, I decided that instead of having my virginity taken from me, I was going to give it to someone I had chosen. And that's exactly what I did. I was barely 15 when I first had sex. I didn't enjoy it. I understood most people enjoyed sex, but for me it was something I HAD to do. It was another thing to add to my list of unpleasant, obligatory responsibilities. It was shameful to me and it made my heart heavy. As a result, shame and guilt around sex would follow me for years and even into my marriage.

Eventually, my family stopped attending church, but I continued to go myself, and I started to enjoy both the service and the people. However, as predicted, my stepfather came for me. Eugene and my mother were having a tough time, so he had moved into his own apartment. One evening he came to our house and said he wanted me to go hang out with him. I declined. My mother then, came to my room and told me to get dressed and go. That was a moment that I will never forget. In that moment it was clear that my mother was mentally unwell. In response to my mother's direction I went to Eugene's apartment. That night he drugged me and raped me at gun point.

I had met my husband at the age of 15 and we were dating when I was raped. I remember both the day that I told him and his response — it was painful for us both. We stayed together, but things got harder for us as the years went on. Despite obstacles and protests from those closest to us we persevered, and we were married in 2003. However, we were a mess, and our marriage was a mess, and it quickly became a source of pain for us both. For me personally, our marriage reinforced my feelings of unworthiness, and

I began to spiral further into depression. That fear, shame, and depression showed on me physically. I saw it clearly for the first time, in the mirror, that fall day that God spoke to me. It showed in the 110 plus pounds I gained, hoping that the extra weight would hide and protect me. It showed in the way I spoke. It showed in my attitude toward men. It showed in how I ate. It showed in the way I dressed and how I went about my days. There it all was, reflected back to me in the mirror. There, in the presence of God, I saw all of the fear and shame, but I also saw truth.

The truth was that my excess weight, my coping mechanisms, and my rough attitude didn't protect me from anything. They couldn't, and didn't, change or heal anything, but God could. For the first time I had hope. I wasn't sure what was in store for me, but I knew that I was not yet who God wanted me to be. After my mirror experience, I began to reach for God more. In Him I began to have a more positive attitude about myself, and I began to exercise and lose weight. Even though I had tried many times before, I knew this time was different. It was different because it was God who compelled me. He gave me some *whys* that energized me and motivated me to be better inside and out. He was doing a work in me, and I was determined to let that work be reflected through me, and on me.

Along my journey, God taught me the strong ties between my mental, spiritual, and physical health. Science may just be catching on, but God began to reveal it to me over 10 years ago, furthermore, those ties were written about in His word long before that. I've spent the better part of the last few years reading science and God's word to gain greater insight into the tie between spiritual, mental, and physical health. As a group fitness instructor I've been able to gain insight into what drives people to exercise. As a personal trainer I've been able to dive more deeply into the mindsets, and lifestyles of my clients. Even throughout churches I've observed that the ties between these three realms of health are evident if one takes the time to look for them. While almost no one would argue the tie between mental, spiritual, and physical health, many fail to recognize the true degree to which physical health is important. Many believers have made their physical health a secondary concern not taking into account that, to God, physical health is a primary concern. God cares about our whole being.

Over the years, I've found that the three reasons why believers lack concern and urgency around their health are: a lack of right thinking, a lack of motivation, and a lack of knowledge. In this book I attempt to address some of the most common hindrances to mental, spiritual, and physical strength/health amongst believers. In this book you won't find a quick fix, a prescribed diet, or a workout plan, because one size does not fit all. What you will find in this book is the word of God because His word does fit all. In His word we can find all things pertaining to life and Godliness (2 Peter 1:3). Through proper study of God's Word, we can learn to think right and find motivation that, in combination with practical tools, will allow us to live life fully. God desires that we live full lives, free lives, through the sacrifice of Jesus. While each of the subjects that I cover (mind, spirit, and body) could command its own book, I hope to impart enough basic knowledge and tools for you start along your own journey to freedom with a strong mind, strong spirit, and strong body.

Part One

Building a Strong Mind

Do not conform to the pattern of this world but be transformed by the renewing of your mind. Then you will be able to test and approve what God's will is – his good, pleasing and perfect will

Romans 12:2 (NIV)

Chapter One

Find a Free Mindset

The sad truth facing most believers today is a feeling of inadequacy or inferiority that manifest in low self-esteem, or self-worth. A lack of self-confidence and a lack of self-love are prevalent among us. The reason many of us lack in these areas is because we have a distorted view of who we are, and flawed thoughts about who we ought to be. Our view will always be blurry, distorted, and dirty when we are trying to look through lenses that don't belong to us, but to others. Likewise, our thoughts about ourselves will always be flawed when we take direction from culture rather than God.

We live in a culture that easily traps us into measuring ourselves against others. From childhood through adulthood, we observe the possessions, decisions, and accomplishments of friends, coworkers, and family. Then, as we observe, we compare, and we begin to feel inadequate. That inadequacy is highlighted for us through the means of social media. We hop on Facebook, Instagram, or other social media apps and watch highlight reels. We see the new home, the new car, the new work assignment, the date night, the weight loss, the perfect family photo... on and on. But what we don't see stamped on the picture is the mortgage or car payment. We don't see the countless hours spent working toward acquiring that work assignment. We don't see the days, weeks, or even months of loneliness that happen in between date nights. We don't see the early morning workouts, the food struggles, or the self-esteem struggles that accompany weight loss. We don't see the hellish daily life of the family with the perfectly groomed children and matching sweaters. We have to be careful, and even protective, about letting the highlights of others influence how we see ourselves. The truth is that many of us spend more time each day scrolling through social media than we do studying God's word, praying, and engaging with other believers combined. It's so common place and so convenient to tap into the lives of others through social media that it slowly, but very efficiently, becomes the thing that we measure ourselves against. Before we even realize it, we have begun trying to measure up against people we may or may not know (some of whom we may not even like). While it isn't healthy for anyone to measure themselves against anyone else's highlight reel, it is especially dangerous for the believer. We, as believers, should instead be measuring ourselves by the word of God and His individual command on our lives.

Because we are relational beings, another measuring stick that we try to stack up against can be the words and actions of those around us. It could be family, coworkers, and/or those we are in service of and with. I see this often in churches. We have to be mindful and loving enough to be aware of how others perceive us. While it is important to be aware of how we are perceived, we must also keep the perceptions of others in their proper place. As believers, we must be careful not to let the perceptions of others overshadow the truth of God's word. When we let perception override truth, we shy away from anything unpleasant. We either don't speak when we should, or we encourage others to say what we don't have the courage to while we sit back and watch. When we allow perception to overshadow God's word, we seldom find ourselves in difficult positions, and consequently, we remain comfortable in our various communities. However, this comfort can cost us commission. We cannot expect greater charge over anything in life if we aren't engaging in good stewardship. Good stewardship is sometimes uncomfortable; it requires: a budget, an eating plan, a firm declaration of God's word — a willingness to stand out against the cultural norm. When a leader, or any believer for that matter, shies away from taking a firm stand on God's word, they unknowingly compromise their integrity while simultaneously diminishing the word of God. While we aren't expected to speak on every offense we see, but if we are in leadership or in personal relationship with someone outside God's will, we should seek to provide guidance. Sacrificing our own comfort for the betterment of those we are in service of and those we are connected to is how we best love one another and reflect Christ. We must be mindful that our action or inaction affects not just us, but also those connected to us, and most importantly, it affects ministry.

In the 13 years my husband has been pastoring I've experienced the discomfort of having to stand "alone". For some years midway through these 13ish years I found myself the object of disapproval. I had inadvertently hurt someone's feelings as I was growing; around that same time, I had to say some things to multiple people that did not go over well. These people banded together and spread nastiness and untruths about me. They attempted to ruin my reputation in order to feel better about their own. The gossip and seemingly constant attacks felt crushing to me; after all, I loved each one of these people. Their perceptions of me began to affect both how I felt about myself, and my confidence level in ministry. I remember, very distinctly, feeling unloved by people I cared for. I remember feeling as if everyone was against me although it was really only 6 people out of more than 150. Some days I was reduced to tears by the attacks and the hateful things said about me; some days I didn't want to be bothered with these people at all.

Yes, these few people mattered. I wanted them to understand that, yes, they were hurting me, but more importantly, they were hurting ministry and dishonoring God by the way that they portrayed me. I wanted to reconcile whatever wrong they felt. I wanted them to understand that I didn't speak to hurt them but for their betterment. I wanted them to be in right relationship with God. It would be many years before they would see what I saw, and even now, I'm not sure that they fully understand.

A turning point in my response to this situation came the day that a deacon unexpectedly approached me with some encouragement and reminders. He pointed out that not only was I looking at a very small contingent of a much larger group, but also that I had let this contingent cause me to lose sight and forget the truth of who I was. These reminders compelled me to remember who I was and what truths I knew. I knew that I was where God wanted me to be. I knew that God had work for me to do right where I was. I knew that even when others would sit quietly and try to seem impartial, I would need to be confident God's word. I showed up and I served because of what I knew, and what I still know to be true: their real issue was not with me, but with God's word. God's word made all the difference; it renewed my mind, refreshed my spirit, and released its strength and power. It allowed me to move forward confidently. Keeping God's truths above the perspective of others allows us to maintain the commission of our lives by:

Remembering who we are

> *But thanks be to God, who always leads us as captives in Christ's triumphal procession and uses us to spread the aroma of the knowledge of him everywhere*
> *2 Corinthians 2:14(NIV)*
> ***

> *But in all these things we are more than conquerors through him who loved us.*
>
> *Romans 8:37(NIV)*

Remembering that we don't know it all

⁸ "For my thoughts are not your thoughts,

neither are your ways my ways,"
declares the LORD.
⁹ "As the heavens are higher than the earth,

so are my ways higher than your ways
and my thoughts than your thoughts.
Isaiah 55:8–9(NIV)
***

For we live by faith, not by sight.
2 Corinthians 5:7 (NIV)

Remembering the promises of God

The Lord makes firm the steps
of the one who delights in him;
Psalm 37:23(NIV)
***

And the God of all grace, who called you
to his eternal glory in Christ, after you
have suffered a little while, will himself

restore you and make you strong, firm and steadfast.

1 Peter 5:10(NIV)

***

I consider that our present sufferings are not worth comparing with the glory that will be revealed in us.

Romans 8:18(NIV)

<u>Vision Check:</u> What are you measuring yourself against? Is it what you see on social media? Is it the approval or disapproval of others? Is it God's word?

Chapter Two

Be Free from Flawed Thinking

In addition to a cloudy or dirty lens, which impedes clear vision, flawed thinking patterns are often the cause of a distorted self -image. Clearing a cloudy or dirty lens requires acknowledging that we have been using the wrong measuring stick to determine our own value; only then can we begin replacing wrong/bad information with the right/good information. While the idea of replacing bad information with good may seem pretty simple, it is often oversimplified. When we struggle with flawed thinking it can be extremely difficult to move beyond the bad information. Flawed thinking is deeply embedded. It's a thought process that has been planted and fed for years.

Our brains thought processes, and the resulting actions that we take, are like roads. The ones most traveled become paved. Of the paved roads, the ones traveled daily, for many years, become highways. The highways become familiar; they may be scary and dark, but the road is straight, and the drive is smooth. Studies have shown that most accidents happen close to home due to relaxation caused by the repetition of the drive. The same is true for the highways we mentally travel – dark they may be, but there is comfort in the repetition. How often will we choose a dark road we know over a lighted street that we don't know? For example, let's imagine a woman who, as a child, consistently witnessed her parents fighting. Scared, she retreated to her room and cried. This happened more and more often as her parents struggled through their marriage. Because retreating and crying was an effective way for her to navigate through her parents' marriage, she began to apply this tactic to other areas of life when tension or conflict occurred. Now she is an adult who avoids any sort of conflict and/or cries each time she is faced with confrontation. Although she may hate her reaction to conflict it has become almost instinctual. With the first few parental fights her brain made a path, over the months a dirt road, over the years a paved road and over decades a highway. We each create highways in our brains. Some serve us well and some lead to accidents.

In my case I had a distorted view of men and relationships. My history of sexual and mental abuse left me with some dark highways of thought. I believed men to be selfish, cunning, and untrustworthy. So, I decided somewhere along the way that the best way to have any relationship with a man was to beat him at his own "game". This way of (flawed) thinking caused me to develop habits and needs (at least in my own perception they were needs) that would ultimately lead to accidents. To have a relationship with a man, I needed to be able to outsmart him. I needed to show less emotion, and less care than he did. I needed to manipulate him to maintain the upper hand. Above all, I needed to constantly remind myself that, no matter what he professed, a man was incapable of truly loving someone, and even *if* he could love someone it would not be me. In my mind I was damaged and dirty. I assumed I would never enter into a relationship in which I could really be me; besides that, I didn't really know who I was anyway so it didn't matter too much. Praise God that despite my flawed thinking and my poor behavior He didn't see me as worthless but as having tremendous value, and He had a plan for me that was so great it surpassed anything I could have ever thought or dreamed of.

When I met my husband at the age of 15, I didn't expect to fall for him like I did. But, I enjoyed talking to him; as we talked his personality drew me in further and further. With this new relationship came excitement and anticipation, however, although the relationship was new, my thought patterns were not. The excitement and butterflies brought by thoughts of him gave way to my more familiar thought patterns. Although I had begun to make new roads; the comfort of my highways was more certain — I knew where they led. I knew how to navigate them, and so I began to consistently remind myself that he had no idea how dirty I was, and yet, I was so captivated by him I really didn't want to tell him and risk his walking away. I was ashamed. As the frequency of phone calls and letters between he and I increased I became increasingly conflicted. Although I knew I was falling in love, and though he had professed his love for me, I held him at arm's length. I felt guilty, ashamed, dirty, and unworthy. Fortunately for me, God was working in me, and for me, before I even began to realize it.

God was in the midst of this relationship from the beginning —no matter how messy we seemed as individuals or as a couple. It seemed as though any time we tried to walk away God would draw us back together; many times the Holy Spirit would compel me to move and behave in ways that were completely outside of the way I had trained myself to. As we continued to talk, write, and visit each other, our connection steadily deepened over the 3 years leading up to our engagement. With much internal dialogue, deliberate action, and a slow, but steady deepening of my relationship with God, I began clearing space for new paths and the grass near the dark highways began to grow over and narrow them back into roads. Those dark highways became less traveled roads, but they were still dark roads that I would struggle with for years to come. I loved my husband deeply and if I wanted to achieve the happy marriage I begun to dare to dream of, I had to pay close attention to the paths, roads and highways I chose. I had to be intentional about being intentional in how I thought. I had to watch my habits of creating distance, following the wrong roads, and fighting until a crash. Seeking God consistently about my marriage and my flawed thinking patterns allowed me to be more open to the conviction of the Holy Spirit. Once convicted, I could either press harder on the gas, stay the course and plow through it, or I could stop and turn back toward those dark, familiar roads. To be honest I did both, and although sometimes I turned back around to those dark, well-paved highways, eventually I would take the long road back to the narrow paths that God was widening for me. It was not easy for me to turn around, or for my husband to always understand and forgive me, but I am grateful to God that he was in the car with me and steadily reminded me in word and deed that God would lead if we would only follow. With God's help and genuine love from my husband I began, and continue, to retrain myself in the way I think.

Although some of us are more easily able to retrain our minds —to force ourselves onto another road or create a new path— some of us have a much more difficult time because our dark highways can be highways of anxiety, depression, abusive thoughts, or addiction, just to name a few. In these cases, formal (clinical) therapy is often a great place to start. Yes, the love of God has the power to lift, and the life and resurrection of Christ can provide joy in any situation, yet we must remember that there is value in medical science and the doctors who practice it. It is extremely hard for someone in the depths of depression to be able to receive the joy of Christ. It can be next to impossible for someone shackled by addiction to receive the freedom being offered by God. If anxiety, depression, or addiction is ruling your thoughts please get some help. No, therapy is not against God's will; it does not rob God of glory. No, it isn't an indication that you are less of a believer. God is able to heal broken bones, however, if you break one don't you visit the ER? God is able to remove cancer; yet, is it not prudent to visit the oncologist? God is able to lower your blood pressure; but, you still need to make dietary changes and in some cases be on medicine. So, yes, God is able to heal your mind and your thinking, however, if your thinking is broken or flawed in some way, you may also need to visit the doctor.

The presence of medical intervention does not equal the absence of God, just as the presence of a storm or struggle does not equate to the absence of faith. We as Christians often praise the duality of Jesus — He was spirit/God enough to walk without sin and ultimately die for ours; yet, He was human enough to feel the same physical and emotional experiences we humans do. Despite His divinity, Jesus felt hunger, thirst, joy, and anger. While praising the duality of Jesus, many believers shame the duality of other believers. The truth is we are both spirit and human. The human part requires us ALL to have medical intervention of some kind. While there are times when Christians have sought counsel because a lack of confidence in scripture or self, most seek counsel in addition to their relationship with God because of anxiety, depression, and/or addiction.

Where there is no counsel, the people fall;

But in the multitude of counselors there is safety

Proverbs 11:14 (NKJV)

Pastors, First Ladies, Elders, Deacons and Deaconesses can all provide wise, sound biblical counsel. Yet, there is still room for secular counseling. Secular counsel coupled with solid biblical counsel works beautifully.

Secular/psychological counsel should challenge negative thought patterns and destructive behaviors while opening the mind and heart to better receive biblical truths. If you struggle with flawed thinking, begin your journey by finding a good counselor/therapist. If you are unsure whether or not you need secular counsel, make an appointment with your pastor. Usually a pastor can tell within a session or two whether or not you are in need of secular or spiritual counsel in order to correct thinking patterns and deeply receive the truth about who God says you are. A correct self-image can only be seen through the clear lens of God. Having a clear self-image and a clear understanding of who God says you are is essential to fighting other mental barriers that impede believers from truly being sound in mind.

Chapter Three

Find Freedom from Fear

Whether an adult or child the feeling of fear is familiar to us all. Some fears are healthy— such as the fear of an automobile accident or of burning our hand on hot coals. Healthy fears are usually the result of parental teaching and experience. In contrast, some fears, although real, are unhealthy to walk in such as: the fear of a natural disaster, fear of losing loved ones or even the fear of dying ourselves. Unhealthy fear is spawned by two things — choices we've made or the interference of Satan. The Bible references fear in two ways, the first of which is "The Fear of the Lord". While non-believers will immediately interpret the fear of the Lord as judgment of lifestyle choices, or as evidence of a list of rules that must be followed, the fear of the Lord should evoke awe and reverence in believers. This fear is a healthy fear; it's a fear that requires us to acknowledge the righteousness and sovereignty of God. The most commonly cited scripture with regard to the fear of the Lord is Proverbs 9:10 which tells us of the importance of fearing the Lord.

The fear of the LORD is the beginning of wisdom, and knowledge of the Holy One is understanding

Proverbs 9:10 NIV

Fearing God compels us to learn more about who He is— about His power and about His sovereignty. When we expand our knowledge of Him, allow Him to impart wisdom and begin to understand better who we are, we will ultimately find: joy, peace, and answers to all of life's questions and obstacles.

The fear of the Lord leads to life;

then one rests content, untouched by trouble

Proverbs 19:23 NIV

The trouble mentioned in Proverbs 19:23 refers to the second type of fear in the Bible, "The Spirit of Fear". I'm sure many of us read this phrase and automatically filled in the blanks with "God has not given us a spirit of fear..."!

For God hath not given us the spirit of fear; but of power, and of love, and of a sound mind.

2 Timothy 1:7

This scripture tells us that that God did not give us the spirit of fear, rather God gives us power over fear; He gives us love over hate and a sound mind over emotions. So, why if we know the scripture, do we still struggle with fear? Usually we struggle with fear because, unless we are feeling overly dramatic, we try to ignore it. We try to move forward despite our fear rather than move forward through our fear. May I suggest that ignoring or pushing past fear is the wrong way to deal with it? Ignoring fear will not overcome it. We cannot conquer what we do not acknowledge. We must identify and acknowledge fear in order to grow and develop into all that we are created to be.

Our ministries, relationships, and loved ones depend on us to grow into who we are designed to be. We cannot reach our full potential and power while walking in fear instead of faith. For years I walked in fear. That fear at times paralyzed me and threatened to break my marriage, my ministry, and my career. Fear of deceit and manipulation caused me to hold my husband at arm's length while I stayed poised for a fight at all times. Fear of being unworthy and unaccepted caused me to shy away from the ministry that God placed within me. Fear of inadequacy caused me to lose years before entering into the career that I was designed for. No matter what the fear is, or what area it attacks, it will cause destruction and loss. We can lose relationships, the opportunity to change lives for God's glory, or years of fulfillment. We must regularly check our lives for fear and its damaging effects.

Identifying and acknowledging fear can be difficult because we don't want to acknowledge that it is present in our lives. We assume that if fear is present, we are somehow failing in our faith walk, but if fear is present, the opposite is likely to be true; we are not failing, but we are flourishing. We are on the cusp of something new. We are on the cusp of something great. The spirit of fear only seeks to derail the plans that God has for us; if we weren't moving toward vision or victory, the spirit of fear would have no need to bother with us. Has God given you a vision that you don't seem to be moving forward in? Fear is, most often, what stops us from moving forward. When we find ourselves with God given vision, but with no progress, we must assess whether or not fear is present.

Fear stops us from leaping to the next level or into a new arena. It stops us from moving forward with pursuing our goals , and instead it causes us to idly wait for God to present our goals to us. Let's say you don't apply for the job that you are technically underqualified for, or if you do, you apply assuming that you won't get the offer. If you follow that thought process, you won't get it. You won't, because your fear has stopped you from believing in yourself. In turn, fear has also stopped you from speaking life over yourself. Fear has stopped you from believing the urging of the Holy Spirit and trusting in God; you have believed the lie that the spirit of fear placed in you.

Consider another example. Perhaps you won't step up to the ministerial calling God has put on your life because you don't speak a particular way or because you believe you will lack support. If you believe that support will be lacking, you will never believe that you have enough-- so, yes, you will lack support. The truth is that support, or the lack thereof, for your calling will become irrelevant because you've already let fear stop you from trying. Fear will consume your conviction and your belief in your calling and ability. Fear is crippling and it will rob you of progress. Maybe you won't go for the degree you really want, embark on a new health and fitness journey, or commit to a new relationship because you fear failure. When fear determines your goals, you will always fail. You will fail because not only have you allowed the spirit of fear to tell you that you will fail, you believed it and began to expect it.

Fear is sometimes masked as "waiting on the Lord". Somehow, we talk ourselves into thinking that if we are met with adversity, or if something is too hard, then God hasn't told us to move yet. That's church cute and it makes us feel good, but it allows us to ignore the fear that is holding us down or keeping us from moving forward. The truth is God already told us that He had more for us. He may have promised a better job, better health, or a better marriage. He promised us all a meaningful, and life changing ministry. He gave us all a sound mind to learn. He has given each of us the strength we need to start our journey. We may not be able to stand immediately in the promise of tomorrow, but we can start to move toward it and prepare for it. If God has given us promise, vision, and direction, we should be walking in it!

We have within us EVERTHING we need to move in the direction that God has given us. When God calls us to something or sends us somewhere, He equips us, and those around us, with everything we need to be successful. Because the life and ministry of each of us is never just about us as individuals, but about the body of Christ as a whole, we are all gifted and equipped differently. God intends for us to work together and support each other -— this is also how we love each other. God is glorified when His people show love to one another and commit to service together. He will divinely connect us to the right people at just the right time if we are moving in the right direction and remain open. God does not idly give direction. He gives direction for our good. He gives direction for the benefit of those around us. He gives direction for His glory. He does not fail, and His plans are solid. Just because we don't know every detail, or understand the fullness of His plans, does not mean that He has failed to plan. He plans for our process because He plans for our victory. Whenever Gods gives vision, He also gives PROvision —"pro" meaning "for". PROvision is everything needed for vision.

Walking in vision— in God's will for us— is perhaps the closest that we can be to whole while we remain on earth. The fruit of walking in vision doesn't just bless us, and those around us, it gives God great glory. It is because of this potential for God to get great glory that fear enters into our lives. Now, I'm not one to blame Satan for everything, but the spirit of fear is from Satan. Earlier in the chapter we looked at 2 Timothy 1:7, "*For God hath not given us the spirit of fear*". That same scripture reminds us that God gave us power, love, and a sound mind; although the spirit of fear is given, it is not given by God. So, the spirit of fear is given, and if it is not given by God, then it must be given by Satan. It is given to prevent us from becoming who we are designed to be.

Fear is a tool of the enemy, however, it is not a sin; fear is an attack. The enemy does not attack what is dormant or dead. He attacks that which is awakening, growing, and flourishing. The enemy attacks either in areas that seem the easiest targets, or in areas that are most threatening to him. The most easily targeted areas are the areas are that vulnerable— areas that are burgeoning. The most threatening areas are areas that give God the most glory. Sometimes one particular area can be both easily targeted and threatening to Satan. When we are granted vision, rarely are we given the full picture, and since we don't have the full picture many of us are walking in burgeoning vision without a clue about how big it really is. Because we don't have the complete picture, it can seem that vision is always evolving, and that makes our area of vision vulnerable. God given vision is always about bringing God glory which makes it a threat to Satan. This is why Satan is about stopping our individual, and our collective, vison walk. The spirit of fear seeks to destroy the faith that makes the vision walk possible.

Because fear can be consuming or paralyzing, it is one of Satan's favorite tools. Believers must be careful not to underestimate the effectiveness of fear. Fear can not only stop us from walking in vision, it can also catapult us in the opposite direction. Fear stirs up adrenaline; this adrenal response has a physical effect on the body. Adrenaline, also known as epinephrine, causes the release of glucose which feeds the flight or fight instinct. When the body doesn't use this glucose, it can leave us feeling restless, irritable, and irrational because of a loss of focus. As a result, we may begin to speak and act in a way that is unbecoming of any believer, and we may begin to backslide not only in our ministries but also in our relationship with God. Remember:

Fear is not sin. Fear is an effective tool of the enemy, used for attack.

Fear is the opposite of faith!

Once we have identified and acknowledged fear, and once we understand that is given by the enemy, we must begin to combat the spirit of fear. If, then, fear opposes and attacks faith, we must combat fear with faith. We must grow in faith enough to overcome the spirit of fear. Romans 10:17 (KJV) says "*So then faith cometh by hearing, and hearing by the word of God*". Fear can only be conquered by faith. As the scripture says faith comes by hearing, so we need to hear from God. The most effective way to hear from God is also the most powerful way to hear from Him— prayer.

Prayer is the modality by which everyone can connect with, and communicate with, God. It is the modality by which we can share with God our desires and our fears. It is the modality that requires us to humble ourselves and causes God to move on our behalf. Psalm 34:4 tells us that God not only will hear our prayer, but that He will also deliver us: "*I sought the LORD, and he heard me, and delivered me from all my fears*". Prayer is the ONLY way to drive out spirits; we are reminded of this in chapter 9 of the book of Mark.

Jesus Heals a Boy Possessed by an Impure Spirit

Mark 9:14-29

¹⁴ When they came to the other disciples, they saw a large crowd around them and the teachers of the law arguing with them. ¹⁵ As soon as all the people saw Jesus, they were overwhelmed with wonder and ran to greet him. ¹⁶ "What are you arguing with them about?" he asked. ¹⁷ A man in the crowd answered, "Teacher, I brought you my son, who is possessed by a spirit that has robbed him of speech. ¹⁸ Whenever it seizes him, it throws him to the ground. He foams at the mouth, gnashes his teeth and becomes rigid. I asked your disciples to drive out the spirit, but they could not." ¹⁹ "You unbelieving generation," Jesus replied, "how long shall I stay with you? How long shall I put up with you? Bring the boy to me." ²⁰ So they brought him. When the spirit saw Jesus, it immediately threw the boy into a convulsion. He fell to the ground and rolled around, foaming at the mouth. ²¹ Jesus asked the boy's father, "How long has he been like this?" "From childhood," he answered. ²² "It has often thrown him into fire or water to kill him. But if you can do anything, take pity on us and help us." ²³ "'If you can'?" said Jesus. "Everything is possible for one who believes." ²⁴ Immediately the boy's father exclaimed, "I do believe; help me overcome my

unbelief!" [25] *When Jesus saw that a crowd was running to the scene, he rebuked the impure spirit. "You deaf and mute spirit," he said, "I command you, come out of him and never enter him again."* [26] *The spirit shrieked, convulsed him violently and came out. The boy looked so much like a corpse that many said, "He's dead."* [27] *But Jesus took him by the hand and lifted him to his feet, and he stood up.* [28] *After Jesus had gone indoors, his disciples asked him privately, "Why couldn't we drive it out?"*

[29] *He replied, "This kind can come out only by prayer"*

This scripture recounts the story of a boy who is seized by an impure spirit. The spirit, although not the spirit of fear, is similar to the spirit of fear. The spirit seizes the boy and causes him to be rigid and unlike the person he was created to be. Although the disciples, due to a lack of faith, had no effect on the spirit, Jesus did; the mere presence of Jesus caused the spirit to convulse within the boy. Jesus then takes the opportunity to tell the father, and those around, that everything is possible for those who believe. He then goes on to rebuke the impure spirit (which we can safely deduce was given by Satan) and cast it out from the boy. Later, when the disciples privately asked Jesus why they were ineffective in driving out the spirit, Jesus told them that this kind of spirit—the kind of spirit given by Satan—can only be driven out by prayer.

Jesus himself teaches us that some spirits can only be driven out by prayer. So, how do we pray to drive out the spirit of fear? God, being a spirit, must be approached in spirit and truth. Thus, making sure our hearts and minds are fully focused on God is important. Prayer that is a matter of action and discipline only—lacking desire and/or a heart after God's own heart—will not drive out this kind of spirit. Likewise, prayer based purely off of momentary discomfort or emotion will not drive out this type of spirit. Driving out the spirit fear requires all of us to use our hearts and minds in combination. Philippians 4:6 is a great scripture to keep in mind when preparing for prayer. It says, *"Do not be anxious about anything, but in everything, by prayer and petition, with thanksgiving, present your requests to God"*.

Effective prayer usually includes 4 components: reverence, repentance, requests and submission.

> ➤ Reverence – acknowledgement of who God is.
> ➤ Repentance – confession of sin and vowing to turn away from it.
> ➤ Requests – whatever is on your heart to seek God for.
> ➤ Submission – yielding to God's will.

We should be specific in our prayers; this is especially true when we are praying out different spirits. When we seek God about the spirit of fear, we need to specifically ask Him to remove it, and we need to pray until our whole spirit is in agreement. When we are praying against a spirit of the enemy, we need to dig deep. We may need to connect with someone else. Note that in the Bible story above, the father keeps reaching out to people until he finds someone who can command the evil spirit. We cannot be afraid to call on our brother or sister in Christ, or our pastor to pray with us. We cannot underestimate the hold of the spirit we are dealing with. We need to be praying in power. We need others who can call out to God on our behalf. Others who are praying with and for us will begin to pour into our spirit. We need the out-pouring of faith to conquer the spirit of fear. This is how we begin to replace the spirit given from Satan with one given from God. The Bible references God as light, and evil as darkness.

And this is the message that we have heard from Him, and announce to you, that God is light, and darkness in Him is not at all;

John 1:5

The spirits of God dwell in light; accordingly, the spirits of Satan dwell in darkness. Light and darkness cannot dwell in the same place.

14(B) and what communion hath light with darkness?

2 Corinthians 6:14 (KJV)

When we pray we are injecting light into darkness; we are injecting faith into fear. As light conquers darkness, so faith conquers fear. Praying for a release from the spirit of fear, coupled with the outpouring of faith is how we conquer the spirit of fear, however, we can't stop there.

Whenever we pray against, or out of, something, we need to fill that space with what we want, otherwise it is left open to be filled by something or someone else that we haven't chosen. We must pray out dark and inject light. We must pray out the spirit fear and inject faith. We need to continue to allow God and His people to pour light and faith into us so that we can remain full. We need to inject power, inject love, and give thanks for a sound mind. As believers we should strive to inject these promises into our daily prayers. Without power, love, and a sound mind we cannot accomplish anything. As we affirm these promises daily in prayer God will GUARD our hearts. He will guard against the attacks of self-doubt, against worry, against darkness. He will guard our hearts against the spirit of fear!

And the peace of God, which transcends all understanding, will guard your hearts and your minds in Christ Jesus"

Philippians 4:7

<u>Vision Check:</u> Is the spirit of fear present anywhere? Is it causing you to be rigid, unmoving, and behaving in a way that is outside of who God created you to be? Take some time to assess whether or not you are moving forward in the direction that God has given you for your life. Check for a lack of movement or joy in your relationships, ministry, and career.

Chapter 4

Find Freedom in Forgiveness

While, for many of us, the spirit of fear can be paralyzing, sometimes the reason for a stagnated or paralyzed life is not fear, but un-forgiveness. Un-forgiveness can be present even when we believe that we have already extended forgiveness, and the offenses that spurred un-forgiveness are seldom as detrimental to us as the effects of the un-forgiveness. Many, if not most, believers struggle with un-forgiveness. While some of us are aware and are struggling to forgive, the rest of us are simply unaware that we are harboring un-forgiveness. There are two basic types of offenses; offenses that are purposely done, and offenses that are accidental. If someone accidentally hurts us, why are we intentionally hurting them by holding a grudge? On the other hand, if someone has intentionally hurt us, why do we believe it's our right to hurt them? Both offenses can cause and lead to un-forgiveness.

When hurt turns to anger and that anger begins to harden our hearts, un-forgiveness begins to take root. Left unchecked, un-forgiveness can cause us not only emotional pain, but spiritual and physical pain as well. It is interesting that we sometimes think we are punishing the person who caused us harm by withholding forgiveness, but the truth is that the punishment we attempt to impart on them is actually passed on to us.

> *For in the same way you judge others, you will be judged, and with the measure you use, it will be measured to you.*
>
> *Matthew 7:2(NIV)*

God does not give us authority to punish others for offenses; in fact, just the opposite is true. The Bible teaches us in the book of Matthew, the 25th chapter, and the 40th verse that whatever is done "to the least of these" is also done unto God. In Deuteronomy 32:25 God declares that vengeance belongs to Him. Ultimately, God will deal with people who have caused us hurt or harm.

While we're trying to even the score by passing judgement and doling out punishment we're adding to our own. Matthew chapter 6 reminds us that we are to forgive as we want to be forgiven; verse 14 and 15 read as follows: *"For if you forgive other people when they sin against you, your heavenly Father will also forgive you. But if you do not forgive others their sins, your Father will not forgive your sins".* By failing to forgive others, we have compromised our own forgiveness. Additionally, Mark 11:24-25 teaches that our unwillingness to forgive will compromise our prayer. Prayer is another foundational principle for all believers because it is our way of connecting and communicating with God. It is also the way that we access forgiveness for ourselves. Ultimately our desire to punish others for hurting us separates us from God, and when we separate ourselves from God who is going to suffer spiritually? Us. And we will suffer even more than we expect. For example:

[23] "Therefore, the kingdom of heaven is like a king who wanted to settle accounts with his servants. [24] As he began the settlement, a man who owed him ten thousand bags of gold was brought to him. [25] Since he was not able to pay, the master ordered that he and his wife and his children and all that he had be sold to repay the debt.

26 "At this the servant fell on his knees before him. 'Be patient with me,' he begged, 'and I will pay back everything.' *27* The servant's master took pity on him, canceled the debt and let him go.

28 "But when that servant went out, he found one of his fellow servants who owed him a hundred silver coins. He grabbed him and began to choke him. 'Pay back what you owe me!' he demanded.

29 "His fellow servant fell to his knees and begged him, 'Be patient with me, and I will pay it back.'

30 "But he refused. Instead, he went off and had the man thrown into prison until he could pay the debt. *31* When the other servants saw what had happened, they were outraged and went and told their master everything that had happened.

³² "Then the master called the servant in. 'You wicked servant,' he said, 'I canceled all that debt of yours because you begged me to. ³³ Shouldn't you have had mercy on your fellow servant just as I had on you?' ³⁴ In anger his master handed him over to the jailers to be tortured, until he should pay back all he owed.

³⁵ "This is how my heavenly Father will treat each of you unless you forgive your brother or sister from your heart."

Matthew 18:23-35 (NIV)

If we choose not to forgive the offenses of others, we cut ourselves off from God AND we will be "handed over" to be tortured. That torture will not necessarily be immediately physical. It is not likely that we're going to be strapped to a chair to be physically tortured, but we may later on experience physical consequences from holding onto to un-forgiveness. The immediate torture that we are "handed over" to begins when we are separated from God. That separation results in fear, anxiety, low self-esteem, depression, loneliness— and the list goes on.

These emotions, when left to fester, can not only imprison us emotionally, they can also imprison us physically. There is a strong tie between our mental or emotional state and our physical well-being. Science is now beginning to confirm what the book of Proverbs has told us all along. Our body responds to what our brain or mind tells it.

A heart at peace gives life to the body, but envy rots the bones

Proverbs 14:30(NIV)

***

Light in a messenger's eyes brings joy to the heart, and good news gives health to the bone

Proverbs 15:30 (NIV)

***

A cheerful heart is good medicine, but a crushed spirit dries up the bones.

Proverbs 17:22 (NIV)

Un-forgiveness costs us so much spiritually, emotionally, and physically that it seems it should be easy for us to let it go. Forgiveness, however, costs us so little that it seems as though it should be easier for us to forgive. After all, we all are, and will continue to be, in need of forgiveness ourselves. Praise God that Jesus paid the debt of our forgiveness on the cross so that we have free and unlimited access to forgiveness. Jesus paid a debt that was ours, and just as our forgiveness cost Him, forgiveness costs us as well.

The first thing that forgiveness costs us is our sense of self-righteousness. The sin and shortfalls of others tend to make us feel self-righteous. The evidence of this self-righteousness is often found in statements like: "I would never...", "At least I...", "I can't believe anyone would..." etc. These types of statements lead us along the road of self-righteousness because we begin to feel superior to the offender. This type of thinking is another way in which we develop a distorted self-image, because we again are measuring ourselves with reference to someone else rather than by God's word! That sense of superiority feeds into the second thing forgiveness costs us – our sense of power.

Oftentimes we hold someone's offense over their head for a while. Many of us find comfort in seeing their remorse— we want to hear it in their apology— we want them to feel the depth of the hurt we feel. Even after moving beyond the initial un-forgiveness we will use a past offense as ammunition for a new fight. Although I'd like to say we walk around with the bullets in our hand ready to load, the truth is many of us are walking around with a loaded gun just waiting to feel justified in drawing it. That loaded gun represents our power. Power is the ultimate thing that forgiveness costs us. Holding that power is like holding our offender's debt; in our minds they have wronged us, they have betrayed us, they have sinned against us, so we are superior to them and they owe us. That power we're holding, that you're holding, that debt you are counting up – IT DOESN'T BELONG TO YOU! When Jesus paid the cost of my debt, of your debt, He also paid their debt.

Forgiveness is a choice. It's a discipline. Romans 12:14 tells us to bless and not curse others.

To bless someone means "to speak well of" them, likewise, to curse someone means "to speak poorly of" them. Un-forgiveness is often the root of curses. If we take every opportunity to share an offense and find ourselves with nothing positive to say about our offender, then it is likely that we are cursing them. We can choose to speak well of someone; we have control of the words we speak. Speaking well of our offender is the first and simplest step towards forgiveness. Note, I didn't say it will be the easiest step, but it will be the simplest. We must refrain from speaking negatively of our offender, and we must resist the urge to rehash the offense. The bottom line is we can't bless, or speak well of, someone and be a gossip. Not only should we bless and speak well of offenders, Proverbs 17:9 encourages us to seek love and actually cover the offense. Covering the offense may seem like it lets the offender off the hook, but what it really does is let us off the hook. Holding a grudge is work. Keeping track of debts owed is work. Staying angry or bitter is work. As we learned earlier in this chapter, this type of work negatively affects your mind, spirit, and body. Don't deceive yourself by believing forgiveness is a release of negative feelings alone, true forgiveness couples that release with action. Forgiveness is a choice. It's a choice to extend God's grace, God's mercy, and God's love to others as freely as God has extended it to us.

We need to liberate the offender, and ourselves, from the debt of the offense. We don't have to hold it. God deals with all of us in His time. Let us speak well of others even if they don't speak well of us. Let us speak well of those who spitefully use us. Let us speak well of those who knowingly hurt us. Let us go even further and begin to cover the offense— cover the offense with love. That doesn't that mean we pretend it hasn't happened. The truth is many of us have experienced things that will stay with us for a lifetime – things that forever change how we view others. In my case, my experiences with abusive men changed the way I view men. And, if I'm completely honest, it hasn't been easy for me to cover *any* offense— even those that really did me no harm beyond hurt feelings. But I chose and choose to forgive. When it is possible I choose to speak well of some of my offenders and in the more extreme cases of offense, when it seems impossible for me to speak well of them, I just don't speak at all.

The truth is that everyone walking the earth has value, everyone has gifting and purpose—they have a right to choose, just as we all do. Today, I use my experiences with being offended to encourage others; outside of that, I try very hard to not just speak well of my offenders, but also to walk and behave in the love God. Being human, I've hurt people, and just as I wanted forgiveness, I try to extend forgiveness. God has challenged and changed me—I've grown and as a result, some things I've said and done in the past I would never even begin to say and do now. We all must allow room for those who have hurt us to make mistakes and to grow from those mistakes. We must recognize that the same blood that cleanses us has the power to clean even those who we deem unforgiveable or unworthy; God can really use anybody. It is not our job to judge who is forgivable and who is not. As believers, we must be careful to measure against God's standard rather than our own. Our own standards dictate who we believe to be forgivable yet, Christ died for us all.

As we strive for freedom through forgiveness, it is important for us to know that forgiveness on our part does not mean that the offender will not face any consequences. Romans 6:23 clearly states, "the wages of sin is death". That death may be a physical death or it may be death to certain opportunities or aspects of life. All of our choices have results, and our poor choices have negative consequences. While we may not experience a physical death stemming from our choices, we experience death in certain areas of life. Emotional or physical affairs often result in the death of a relationship. Gambling often results in the death of financial health. Poor communication with a spouse often leads to the death of real intimacy. Betrayal of a friend may lead to the death friendship— on and on. However, suffering through these consequences does not release us from our call to forgive. The longer we choose to not forgive, the more suffering the we open ourselves to because we are outside of the protection of God. Remember, the heart that we use to deal with others is the same heart that we receive from God; He extends forgiveness as we extend forgiveness.

While forgiveness does cost us our false sense of self-righteousness and our sense of power, the freedom found in forgiveness is far greater than the constraint. We need to be careful and honest about the un-forgiveness we feel. The longer we remain in un-forgiveness the harder it will be to walk in freedom. Consider the example of those who have experienced incarceration. The longer that individuals are incarcerated, the harder it is to adjust to their new freedoms when they are released. When individuals are imprisoned for long enough, they can sometimes stop being people who have spent time in prison and instead become prisoners. God does not want us to be prisoners. God wants us to live free, not to be bound physically, emotionally, or spiritually. Too often we allow ourselves to be in bondage in one area or another. We fail to recognize the harm we do to ourselves, and how closely intertwined our physical, mental, and spiritual beings are. Being free by forgiving others allows us experience the joy and peace that God has promised. Being freed by forgiving allows us to love others in a way that leads to healthier and happier relationships. Being freed by forgiving allows us to be available for advancement

and vision. God has purpose and use for our lives—
something great and greater than us. Even before we
see the vision there is already provision ready for us
to use right where we are. We need to seek our
freedom through forgiveness so we can ultimately
flourish in God's provision and vision for our lives!

Vision check: Are you harboring un-forgiveness?
When a good friend —someone who you share your
secrets with—brings up someone who has wronged
you caused you pain, how do you respond?

Do you find yourself re-hashing or replaying events to
see what happened within a relationship?

If you were in position to help that person/people, who
offended you, would you? If you answer yes, would it
be out of obligation or out of love?

Chapter 5

Evolve Beyond your Emotions

Our emotions are one of the most common excuses given for why we don't do the things that either we ought to do, or that we are called to do. Yes, we know we should forgive and we even have strategies to help us, but we are hurt so, we don't want to forgive. Our hurt feelings and self-pity allow us to rehash events in an effort to feel justified in some way. Our pain and anger allow us to blow up, speaking and behaving in ways that warrant repentance. Our despair and sadness allow us to overspend, either in a mall or on an experience, in order to take our minds off of our problems. Our feelings of condemnation and shame allow us to separate from others and be reclusive and uninvolved. Despite what we know we should do, we often allow our emotions to justify acting irrationally. It's not surprising that this is more and more common. We live in a "#inmyfeelings" world that tells us we should allow our feelings to determine our actions, but, I beg to differ. We should take action based on how we are being led by the Holy Spirit who dwells within each of us. Now our emotions— our feelings— *DO* matter. However, while our feelings do *influence* the choices we make they should not *rule* our behavior. If we allow negative emotions such as loneliness, rejection or sadness to rule us, they will drive us away from God and our God-given purpose. The reality is just because we feel a certain way about someone or something doesn't mean that we are right. Being happy in a relationship does not mean we are in the right relationship. Being upset with someone who has challenged us doesn't mean that what they said isn't true. Feeling lonely doesn't mean we are really alone or that we have to stay alone. Emotions are often based on surroundings and interactions with people; because our environment or company is subject to change so are our emotions. Emotions are too fickle and temporal to base any decision on.

Our emotions are something to be managed, however, they are not something to be conquered or overlooked— they are a gift. While we should not use our emotions to try to authenticate truth or manipulate others, we should put them to use. Our feelings are usually strong indicators of what's going on in our hearts and minds. They can provide us insight if we dig deeper and try to discover what has triggered a particular emotion. Our feelings or emotions are the symptom and not the source. Good feelings and bad feelings, positive emotions and negative emotions can hinder our walk and spiritual growth. Negative feelings about a particular person can stop us from sitting under and submitting to sound biblical teaching. For instance, not liking a particular teacher, for personal reasons, may compel us to skip their lesson and miss a message from God. In a similar manner, positive feelings, evoked by uplifting worship music, can compel us to sit Sunday after Sunday in a church that does not challenge us to grow. Although these examples are of negative and positive feelings respectively, both feelings produced the same outcome— a missed opportunity for growth.

As we grow up, our parents and/or lives teach us that not everything will feel good. It is vitally important that we remember this lesson. As we mature as believers we should understand that growth comes with change, and change comes with challenge. If faith in God ensured that we were always going to feel good, then there would be no need for faith at all. If God meant for us to be ruled by and respond only to our emotions, He would not have given us His written word to live by. Much of the sin we fall into is because we are submitting to our feelings. If one finds they are "falling out of love" with their spouse and cruising toward divorce, it's often because they are operating based on negative emotion within their marriage rather than actively pursuing the promise of God within and for the marriage. An adulterous affair is usually the result of someone operating out of a feeling of inadequacy in some area. If someone repeatedly finds themselves waking from a drunken stupor, it's likely because some negative emotion is driving them there. If someone often finds themselves speaking poorly or being a gossip, they are usually driven by emotion. Operating out of emotion is the most common source of sin and sin often feels good, or right, in the moment; but, we as believers are aware, on some level, of when our behavior does not line up with God's will for us. Although we may not overcome every emotion, we must begin to evolve beyond them. Understanding who we are and who we are created to be, setting our minds and hearts after God's, and determining to walk uprightly is the beginning of how we start to evolve. When we have good solid knowledge and when we begin to think right, we can take the right physical action and do right. The more often that we think and do right, the more of a habit it will be, and it we will begin to feel right.

Vision Check: Are you being led by the Holy Spirit, or by your emotions? Hint— direction from the Holy Spirit will ALWAYS line up with the word of God.

Part Two

Building a Strong Spirit

"I am the vine; you are the branches. If you remain in me and I in you, you will bear much fruit; apart from me you can do nothing.

John 15:5 (NIV)

Chapter 6

Strengthen through Study and Devotion

In ministry, I have found one the most commonly confessed shortcomings to be a lack of regular Bible study. Consuming God's word is how we nourish our soul. In order to thrive and produce good fruit for our lives and for those around us, we have to be careful of what we feed our spirit. Too often we are fed poison— by what we choose to watch, read, and listen to— without realizing it. The world will tell us that there are no hard lines, that gray areas exist, however, God's word tells us otherwise. In God's word, it is black or white, right or wrong, love or hate. While some decisions may be hard and some life decisions may have more than one right answer, questions that involve morality, behavior, and the treatment of others do simply boil down to what God would ultimately have us to do. It's also prudent for us, as believers, to understand that in some cases inaction is just as harmful/bad/wrong as taking the wrong action or making the wrong decision. James 4:17, reminds us that it is a sin for us to know the right thing and still fail to do it. We can either do what is right or do nothing. We can either give a firm Christ-like answer or avoid the question. We can either show love or allow hate.

The body of Christ has become too saturated with the influences of the world. We accept things that are not Godly simply because they're normal or because we don't to be seen as outcasts, hypocrites, or judgmental. We often use the fact that God gave each of us free will as a reason to avoid being honest with others; therefore, avoiding any accusations of being hypocritical or judgmental. This avoidance is dangerous because it not only allows our brothers and sisters in Christ to remain outside of God's will, but it also compromises God's word while simultaneously compromising our own integrity and ability to effectively evangelize. God, indeed, has given us all free will, and the people of the secular world have a right to choose how they will live their lives. Likewise, we as the people of God have a right to choose how we will live our lives, however, along with that right, we, as believers, also have a mandate. Our mandate as believers is to evangelize, to create more disciples, to share God's love, and to teach others how to live in right standing with him. Unfortunately, we often do a poor job of representing God. Often the reason for poor representation is the manifestation of three things.

1. We are too self-righteous. We view our mandate as a reason to beat people with God's word and standard – usually in a way that is both favorable to us and lacking love for them. We use God's word to back up poor politics. We use God's word to belittle others while setting ourselves up for leadership positions within the church. We use God's word against others so that we feel better about ourselves. What is most disheartening about this is that although we are attempting to represent God, we are actually accomplishing the opposite.

2. We lack real understanding of God's word and therefore, we have poor application and discipleship results.

3. We are so complacent in our relationship with God that we lack zeal, conviction, and any sense of urgency. The lack of zeal, conviction, and urgency will make us more accepting of the world and its blurred lines— so much so that people don't even know we are believers. Complacency in our relationship with God will result in complacency with the world.

Unfortunately, members of the body of Christ have also been fed poison by other believers— be they friends, deacons, elders, or even pastors. These people can mean well; they can mean to encourage us, to pour into us, to steer us closer to God. While their hearts and intentions can be pure and Godly, some may unknowingly cause harm instead of the good they intend. The problem is even well-meaning believers can misuse, misquote, or misunderstand God's word. And honestly, consuming this poison is our fault. Why? Because we don't know enough of God's word for ourselves to test the "encouragement" that we are fed. This is further complicated when we are happy to sit at just anyone's spiritual table to be fed. While there are lots of great teachers and speakers, chances are if we consistently expose ourselves to different teachers and speakers, eventually we will hear poor theology or doctrine. If we regularly consume meat prepared by various cooks with various preferences, we will eventually encounter meat that isn't fully cooked, a chicken breast lacking a firm texture, a steak that is a bit too rare, or a beautifully seared pork chop that is slightly too pink. The question is— will we realize it?

Steaks in particular can be ordered at multiple temperatures and still be safe to eat; however, there are temperatures that even though safe, are not recommend for regular consumption. Furthermore, if we have steak that is too rare, even once, it can cause us to be sick. The best way to determine which steak temperature is best for us is to cook some steak at home. While preparing food at home may be more time consuming, it's often the healthiest food we can have. Cooking at home is usually more time consuming because we have to figure out: what we want to cook, what ingredients we need, how to cook them, and for how long we need to cook them. Cooking steak at home ensures quality control. It's exactly the same for what we feed our spirit. Ensuring the quality of the spiritual nourishment we receive from others also begins with learning to nourish our own spirit. For every believer, the Bible is the best source of spiritual nourishment. The Bible contains information about what to cook, the ingredients needed, and the appropriate process.

All of the instruction we need for a Godly, healthy life, as well as the answers to all of life's questions—simple and complex—can be found in God's word. Most people, at some point or another, will have questions about life such as:

"Why am I where I am?" - *Matthew 28:19-20*

"Why is there so much evil in the world?" - *1 John 4:8*

"How do I handle my hurt?" - *Ephesians 4:26*

"How do I manage my money?" - *Proverbs 22:7*

"How can my marriage be better?" - *Ephesians 5:25-28*

"How can I be happy or joyful?" - *Colossians 3:23*

For every question, the Bible provides an answer, and these are just a few of my go to scriptures. The Bible is a collection of history, instruction, and story that can be applied to multiple areas of our lives. The thing I love most about the Bible is that while there are so many stories, direct instructions, and historical accounts that we can use to find the answers we need, the answers are always consistent. God's word and His ways are consistent with who He is. The hallelujah about this is that God is faithful. He is faithful to His people. Hebrews 13:5 reminds us that God will never leave us or forsake us. God's faithfulness to us is why He has left us with His written word. In God's word we find all, pertaining to life, that we need to know as believers. We learn how to achieve peace by learning how to discern spirits and situations. We learn who we are and who God created us to be as we learn more about who God is through His word. In God's word we find salvation, victory, peace, strength, joy, growth, and guidance.

Alright, so now that we know we need to study God's word, the question becomes how do we effectively study God's word? Many of us have tried to get into a regular, personal practice of study and have failed. We may have tried reading the Bible straight through and retained nothing. Perhaps we tried the Bible in a year model, but quickly found that it just became a reading assignment or a mindless exercise as soon as we hit all those "begat(s)", and so, again, we retained nothing. It's possible that we tried several daily plans (including the infamous Daily Bread) but again fell off and/or retained very little. Sometimes these plans don't work because our approach is wrong. Even though we mean to grow closer to God, we wrongly think that we need to memorize scripture, or that we need to finish all of the passage, or that we need to adhere to a schedule of some sort. The truth is we don't need to memorize scripture, we should take time to meditate and sit with anything that intrigues or convicts us, and our schedules don't matter that much to God.

I believe there are several key factors for starting and maintaining a healthy Bible Study habit.

1. Understand that learning and studying God's word doesn't need take or last an hour or more.

   Somehow—maybe from another believer who has been saved since the day before forever—we get it into our minds that the length of time we spend studying God's word matters, but it doesn't—at least not to God. I remember a period of time during which I was spending two to three hours a day reading the Bible. I learned nothing. *Nothing.* I could barely recall what I read one day to the next let alone the next week. My intention was good. I wanted to learn about God; I wanted to be closer to Him, but my approach was wrong. My approach was wrong because my preconceived notions were wrong. When our approach is wrong, our intentions do us no good. We can intend to show someone love, but if we don't do it before they are gone, our intentions don't matter. We can intend to study for a test, but if we don't do so before testing time comes, then our intentions don't matter. We can intend to exercise, but at the end of the day our intentions don't matter without action; our intentions won't make us stronger.

For as well intentioned as I was in trying to study God's word, all I really did was waste time. I could cross my personal Bible Study off my checklist, and that did make me feel good for a little while, but, as the words I read escaped my memory, so did that good feeling. The pressure of studying for an allotted amount of time and the idea that I needed to read all of God's word within a designated schedule was extremely overwhelming. Starting anything new and important can be scary or overwhelming. Studying and understanding God's word can be overwhelming for any of us when we are just getting started even without the added pressure of schedules and time.

The thing is, no matter how long or how deeply we study God's word there will always be more that we can learn. There will always be another spiritual challenge, another nuance, another verse, or another story that we missed. God doesn't need us to know it all, he simply wants us to seek after Him. As our spirits begin to grow, so will our spiritual hunger; thus, causing us to naturally seek out more of God. Our learning and study habits will continue to evolve as we grow. We may also experience times when we scale back or slide back from our steady incline—this is quite common and, in my opinion, a part of the journey. In fact, I've yet to meet a solid Christian who hasn't experienced moments or periods of waning in their spiritual lives. The key is not to stay there, being connected to, and surrounding ourselves with Godly people and environments will often pull us out of a spiritual slumber.

2. Set aside time specifically designated for God and for learning who He is.

Setting aside time for God and for learning His word makes God a priority. It turns our intention into action, and grabs God's attention. While the length of time is secondary, setting aside time for God is primary. It's true that God doesn't measure time the way we do, He does clearly put emphasis on time. God created day and night; His word contains multiple references to seasons. Moreover, God even set time aside for us to rest. Furthermore, Psalms 90:12 reminds us to number our days to acquire a heart of wisdom, while Colossians 4:5 reminds us to walk in wisdom towards outsiders and make the best use of our time. If you've been in church for at least 2 weeks, then I'm sure you've heard that "God is always right on time". Time is important to God and sacrificing our time to Him demonstrates our love and commitment to Him. After all, how can we show someone we love them if we are unwilling to spend time with them?

I am a firm believer that everyone makes time for the things and the people that are important to them. We've all said or heard the excuses: "I work so much", "I have so little time left at the end of the day", "I can't find extra time to spend in study or prayer". Why is it that we don't say "I work so hard and have so little time left over that I can't go on vacation, or I can't watch TV, or I don't have time to gossip"? Within these questions is both the problem and the answer. We want to give God the leftover! This mind set of giving God our leftover is dangerous.

²ᴮNow Abel kept flocks, and Cain worked the soil.³ In the course of time Cain brought some of the fruits of the soil as an offering to the Lord.⁴ And Abel also brought an offering—fat portions from some of the firstborn of his flock. The Lord looked with favor on Abel and his offering,⁵ but on Cain and his offering he did not

*look with favor. So, Cain was very angry, and
his face was downcast.*

*⁶ Then the Lord said to Cain, "Why are you
angry? Why is your face downcast?⁷ If you do
what is right, will you not be accepted? But if
you do not do what is right, sin is crouching at
your door; it desires to have you, but you must
rule over it."*

Genesis 4:2-7 (NIV)

While most would focus in on Cain's offering
and try to discern why God did not accept his
offering, I'd like to focus in on Abel's offering.
Abel brought an offering from the first born of
his flock. He did not wait until he had
established what he considered a sizable flock
before giving his offering, but instead he gave
God the firstborn or the first part of the flock.
He did not give God what he felt he could spare,
or what was leftover; he gave God the best he
had, and he did so with the right heart and
mindset. The scripture is clear that God looked
upon both Abel and his offering with favor.

When we offer ourselves or our time to God, we must do so with the right mindset, thereby ensuring we are giving Him our best. God will not accept an offering, no matter how good it seems, if we give that offering with a poor heart or mindset.

The latter part of the scripture above clearly indicates God's displeasure not just with Cain's offering, but also with Cain. Whether God's displeasure stems from Cain's offering or Cain's actions, we can be sure that a poor mindset is at the root. A poor mindset will always lead us to poor decisions and poor behavior, and poor decision-making invites sin to be crouching at the door. But, just as God commanded Cain, we are to rule over sin. Falling short is not an excuse to stay in, or be complacent with, sin. Giving God our leftover offering of time means that not only are we wrong but, we are also going to struggle more with sin. God indeed wants our first; He wants our best. Practically speaking, this doesn't mean our offering of time has to be as soon as we wake in the morning—although that works for many of us. Giving God our best and our first means that when we plan the day and what we want to accomplish, our the first priority is God; so, setting aside time for God, whether 15 minutes or an hour, is the first thing we schedule. We should schedule it at the time when we are most clear headed—when we can shut everything and everyone else out. It should be scheduled for a time when we can be without any distractions. We must give God the best and the first. For me personally, the best time for me to offer God is after I've been up for some time, but before I start my day. The reality is, if I try to sit on the edge of my bed just after waking, I am blurry minded and likely to lie back down. However, if I get up, shower, and dress first, I can then shut myself in my room on my bed and give God my full attention, because I am awake. I've not yet left my room so, I am not distracted with all the to-dos waiting outside my door. My family is either still asleep or informed that I am studying or in prayer. In order to accomplish this, I had to make a few things happen. I had to plan to get up a bit earlier so I go to bed earlier— *we must manage our time.* My family knows and respects my habits— *we must be clear with those we live with and, in some cases, set boundaries.* I plan to focus on God alone each morning so each night I make sure my room is in order— *we must create an orderly environment in which to seek God.* It's hard to focus when you are still sleepy, when your family is calling for your attention or when you are staring at a pile of laundry and/or a stack of bills. Eight times out of ten one of those distractions will seep into your thought process. Giving God our best and first also means we turn our intention into action, beginning with preparation.

3. Study for application not memorization.

Too often we, believers, get caught up in our own expectations of ourselves and of others. These expectations can start out seeming reasonable for example, the fact that God wants us to know His word. While this is true, we have simplified this to an exercise that enables us to quote scripture verbatim. Let's be real—a good portion of what is regularly quoted is either quoted incorrectly or used out of context. Even the assertion that God wants us to know His word is only half of His expectation. He not only wants us to know His word, Psalm 119:11 tells us that He wants us to hide it in our hearts," that we might not sin against Him". Often, we study or read God's word simply to memorize it. Further, we can't even claim that we hide it in our brains, much less our hearts! Instead, we are eager to share our knowledge of it before we forget. We keep our newly memorized scripture in the forefront of our brains ready to roll off the tongue should a conversation even come close to being relevant. We can get good at storing up a lot of scripture within our minds (which is great, we should know and be able to reference Gods word), but the problem is that we sometimes miss the second half of God's instruction to hide it in our hearts. Hiding God's word in our heart will compel us to live it rather than just quote it. I've found that one of the best ways to get God's word into my heart is to ascertain how (within its context) I can effectively apply it to my life. When I study God's word I study for application not recitation.

One of the first things I recommend to any new believer is to read a Bible translation that he or she can understand. While traditionally, the King James Version (KJV) has been used in the churches I've attended, when I study the Bible, I generally start with the New International Version (NIV) simply because I can read it more easily. Because I'm not trying to translate words or sentences when I read the NIV, it's easier for me to digest. When I first began studying God's word on my own, I would get tripped up on some of the language and get frustrated by having to internally convert every "thee", "thou", and "thy" that I came across within the KJV so I switched to the NIV. I still use KJV when I want to dive into a particular word or scripture more thoroughly, however, it's more my secondary reference than my first. After all, why should we struggle when we don't have to? Yes, as we move further away from the original languages that the Bible was written in we lose some things in translation, but this is true for the KJV translation as well. So, when studying to apply, a more modern translation of the Bible may be more readily retained.

When studying the Bible, it is important to understand not only the language, but also the context of each scripture. While it is okay to quote or reference part of a verse, it is not okay to misuse part of the verse. For example, when someone is struggling, we often use "all things work for the good" to provide encouragement. Yes, that is Bible, however, saying that to a non-believer is vastly different from saying that to a believer. The entirety of that quoted scripture from Romans 8:28 (KJV) says, "*And we know that all things work together for good to them that love God, to them that are called according to his purpose*". Now, I'm just simple enough to take the Bible as it's written. While the Bible contains depth beyond what any one person could possibly take in, much of the direction given to God's people is simple. In this case, the promise that all things work together for our good is for those of us who love God and walk in His purpose for our lives. There are plenty of people whom I love dearly that don't carry that same promise, so if I were to encourage them with this scripture not only would my use of scripture be irresponsible, I'd be lying. Yes, God loves everyone, but not everyone loves Him, and so using this promise to encourage people who are outside of God's will and/or purpose for them is a misuse of this scripture. This is why it is of the upmost of importance that we take the time to fully understand scripture and its context before we begin to apply it.

Applying the word of God to our lives daily and seeing the fruit of that application daily will encourage us to continually go deeper into God's word, and this will result in it being hidden in our hearts. One might argue that we should believe first and then it becomes habit— I believe that the process of learning and application is circular but that it initially starts with a personal struggle of some sort that first compels us to seek God. Many of us become believers after finding God in our most desperate moments. We try God, find Him good, and our faith and trust are deepened each time God makes Himself known. I recognize that this may be challenging to some because many believers are taught, or raised, to never question or test God. To be clear, I'm not suggesting that we should challenge or tempt God, but I am suggesting that we test or try God. I am saying that those of us who trust in Him for ourselves, and not by way indoctrination, have at some point tested or tried God.

I met God in one of the darkest moments of my life. I was sitting on my bathroom floor with a bottle of pills when He intervened.

Although I had been going to church for years, God was not ruling in my life at that time. I was ruling my life, and as a result my life was a mess; my thought processes were flawed and messy, my emotions were tumultuous and messy, and my marriage was severely strained and messy. There I was on my bathroom floor having cried so much that I was almost catatonic. As I sat there searching myself I remembered some of the truths of God; He is ever-present, all knowing, and capable of saving anyone. I audibly spoke less than three words to God not really expecting an answer or a result. But, God. God answered and made Himself known to me that very moment. He responded so plainly that there has never been any question or doubt that it was Him. God saved my life, not just my spiritual life, but also my physical life. He saved all of me that day. I have never been the same, and I'll never forget that day. God cares about our whole being— mentally, spiritually, and physically. So, yes if you're unsure or dealing with unbelief in any area big or small, try God. Find a scripture, find a promise, and dare to try Him. Scripture not only teaches us, but it will also come back to our remembrance and provide us with hope when we hide it our hearts.

For everything that was written in the past was written to teach us, so that through the endurance taught in the Scriptures and the encouragement they provide we might have hope.

Romans 15:4 (NIV)

***

"Oh taste and see that the Lord is good!"

Psalm 34:8 (NIV)

4. If you're hungry for God, I highly recommend starting with a guided devotional.

So often, the biggest hurdle to growing closer to God is developing the habit. We want to study more. We want to pray and connect with God more, yet we struggle with getting started. I find that these attempts usually follow the same pattern. We begin with pairing our intention with action by setting up our space and reserving the time. Next, we rise early and get started. Monday – Friday of week one we are consistent. Then the weekend comes along and we are a bit shaky, but we may push through into the next week and so on. But, as this pattern continues we eventually fall completely off. Sometimes we fall off because we aren't realistic about our schedules or what we've planned to accomplish; this is where a devotional comes in. Daily devotional guides generally include a scripture accompanied by a short reading, points to focus on to apply to our daily life, and/or points that we may need to add to our prayer life. These guided devotionals are great for starting a new practice of personal Bible study and even prayer because they generally don't demand a lot of time. Many require less than 10 minutes with journaling; the time that is unpredictable is the time that will be spent in prayer.

Although guided daily devotionals are a great way to set the tone for the day ahead, choosing one can be quite overwhelming. In fact, there are thousands of devotional books, apps, and guides within apps. One helpful method for filtering through these options is to first consider that many guides are designed to be worked through in a set amount of time. Most of these options tend to be 7, 10, 21, or 40 days in length, and most people tend to gravitate toward a 21-day guide. I believe that this may be because 21 days seems like a significant amount of time without being overwhelming. And, after all, doesn't it take 21 days to build a habit anyway? Well, yes and no. If the habit that we want to pick up is as simple as drinking a glass of water first thing every morning, then yes, 21 days of intentional practice may suffice. However, I believe that goals that require more energy and thought take longer before becoming a habit because they require more discipline. If the goal is to build a habit of regular study and prayer, I would recommend starting with a 40-day devotional. A 40-day devotional, which is nearly double a 21day devotional, requires more commitment, and is more likely to develop into a habit. After years of struggle trying to develop a regular habit of study and prayer, a 40-day guided devotional, combined with my deep desire to be closer to God finally helped me build the regular study and prayer habit that I wanted to achieve. I then followed those 40 days of guided devotion with my own unguided prayer time, for 3 weeks, before starting a new devotional and now my spirit craves that connectedness daily. Now, my day is off unless I've spent some time with God before I leave my house. Even spending just a few minutes connecting with God and His word makes all the difference.

Many of us do have time devoted to connecting with God and to studying His word. On the surface, and technically, we are all good. We have regular study and prayer. We know a little bit of Bible. We attend church and corporate prayer and study. We tithe and we serve. Yup, we got this together. Some of us have even had it together for years. So where is the problem?

Often the biggest obstacle to personal and corporate growth among God's people is complacency. While we want to develop the habit of regularly connecting with God, we need to be careful that we don't let our relationship with God become just another habit. As I pointed out earlier, reading God's word and hiding it in our hearts are two different things. The same is true for some of our habits; we all have mindful and mindless habits. For example, one or two generations ago, our parents may have taught us to pray before each meal thereby creating a habit for us. This habit is great as long as it's a mindful habit in which we are actually offering thanks and not simply recital.

Never be lacking in zeal, but keep your spiritual fervor, serving the Lord.

Romans 12:11 (NIV)

Romans 12:11 says that we should be careful to not be lacking in zeal or spiritual fervor; so, we must guard against complacency. As I've mentioned before, we cannot guard or overcome anything that we do not acknowledge. Acknowledging complacency requires some maturity because it implies something negative about something that we feel okay about. The reality is that complacency in our relationship with God (or any other divine relationship placed within our lives, such as marriage) is a dangerous thing. It's my opinion that complacency leads to death. Being complacent in any area of our life means we are content with how things are and see no reason to push for anything greater. The truth is, no matter how great a thing is, it can always be better. Consider the analogy of a tree. When we are complacent, we like the fruit that we have produced, and we see no reason to do the work of cultivating new fruit. We are complacent, even happy, and oblivious to the fact that our fruit is dwindling, or rotting. Sure, some of our fruit may have been shared and consumed as it should be, however, our complacency tends to leave us holding a good portion of fruit—admiring it, talking about it, but not using it. What we are missing is the fact that fruit that is not consumed will eventually rot. And, the lack of consumption of our fruit often leads to the lack of effort needed to cultivate and produce new fruit. Complacency causes us to stop producing new fruit, and though we may yet still live, we eventually become barren. When we as individuals become barren, God must begin to prune us and if we still do not produce we will be cut down.

If zeal is lacking in your relationship with God, in your study, or in your prayer life, then you may have become complacent. I have found that the best way to revive zeal is fasting. Fasting is giving up something that is both, part of your daily life and also challenging to abstain from. The majority of fasts typically involve giving up food during certain hours of the day, giving up certain foods, or eating according to a plan such as "The Daniel Fast". Although fasting is usually associated with a lack of food there are plenty of other things one could fast from: TV, social media, shopping etc. While fasting is good for our spirit-person, it is also beneficial to our physical-person. Still, it's important to remember two important things when it comes to fasting. The first thing to keep in mind is that a fast is not a diet. You may lose weight while fasting and while for many that is great— perhaps even necessary— if at the end of the fast the biggest movement was on the scale, then you did it wrong. If there is minimal or no spiritual movement, you did it wrong. What this type of result shows is that the fast, although started with the right intention, morphed into a fast that was about you rather than about God and your relationship with Him. Fasting should be about drawing closer to God and not about getting closer to a smaller pant size.

The second thing to be mindful about when fasting is that you cannot "fast" from things that God did not intend for you to have to begin with. You can't fast from any addiction; God wants you to break any addictions. Going 10, 21 or 40 days without a cigarette, without drunkenness, without sex outside the confines of marriage, without pornography, etc. should be considered a win if going without those things is a struggle (because they are coping mechanisms), but, while it's a win to break away from these things, they are behaviors that need to be stopped. Fasting from something suggests an intention to pick it back up. Though God's grace, mercy and goodness saves everyone, you should never plan to revive behavior that God has already delivered you from.

Avoiding the common pitfalls of fasting is easiest done by choosing the right fast. Try to choose one that is clearly structured and speaks as much to your spirit as it does to your mindset and to your body. One of my favorite ways to fast is in combination with a guided devotional. Just as there are daily devotional books, there are devotional books that are meant to be combined with fasting. The combination of fasting in a way that requires real sacrifice and challenging study is extremely effective, and it is one of the best ways to revive a complacent spirit.

<u>Vision check:</u> Do you have regular time devoted to learning more of God's word? If you do, are you zealous in your effort to learn and apply God's word and direction?

Chapter Seven

Strengthen through Prayer

When I first met my husband, I was fifteen and he was seventeen; I lived in Scranton, PA and he in Ithaca, NY. I love to look back on our relationship and how it grew. We were young and "in love" living two hours away from each other. Keep in mind this was in the late 90s. We still used landline phones and paid for long distance by the minute. Having a pager was the thing back then, and cell phones were emerging, but were still far from the norm. I remember sending love letters almost weekly, and I remember the exciting fifteen-minute calls that we managed to plan and afford every seven to ten days. It's interesting how as our relationship intensified, so did the frequency of our communications, and as our conversations became more profound, the depth of our relationship also became deeper. Going deeper into relationship shifts conversation from light or temporary things, such as how attractive we find the other and plans for the weekend, into more long-term things such as understanding the heart and desires of the other and making plans for the future. Now, having been together more than twenty years (married for over fifteen) I can definitely say that the health of our relationship is directly affected by, and reflected in, how we communicate. Effective communication enables us to connect with each other, align our hearts and minds, and to take the opportunity to hear from each other. This type of communication works for us because, we when we are truly aligned and connected, our goals and priorities are also aligned. With God as the center of our relationship, we have never encountered an obstacle that we were not able to overcome.

Regular and open communication is the basis and lifeline for any healthy relationship. This is especially true for our relationship with God. Regularly communicating with God will deepen our relationship with God and that depth will then begin to be reflected in our prayers. Acquiring depth in our prayer life requires being able to really connect with God, align with God, and hear from God. So, when we pray we ought to:

1. Pray to connect

Prayer is the most effective way to connect with God. When we approach God, we must do so with a humble heart. We must pray acknowledging Him for who He is and ourselves for who we are. This means that for us to connect with Him, we must also address the thing that separates us from Him— sin. It was man's sin that created a divide between man and God and Jesus' sacrifice that ultimately bridged that gap. Jesus provides for us the path to use to go before the Father, however, something is required from us as well. Jesus didn't just die so that we can commune with the father; He died so we no longer need to offer sacrifice before communing with Him. Jesus, being the perfect sacrifice, died taking on our sins so that we could have access to God the Father. Because His blood was shed to cover our sin we must approach God gratefully, humbly, and with repentance. Too often we say "Jesus paid it all" and gloss right over our sin, and our responsibility in our sin, expecting no consequences. Isaiah 59 reminds us that unconfessed sin causes God to turn His face from us and that God will only come as the redeemer to those who repent. If we truly seek to connect with God, we must confess our sin, and then go further by repenting.

There is a difference between confession and repentance. Confession is acknowledging, and perhaps feeling guilt for, the sin. Repentance is one step further than just acknowledging sin, in that we not only acknowledge our sin, but we are actively turning away from it. Repentance is the difference between simply acknowledging the wrong of living in sin, or being shacked up, and taking the steps to separate until being married. Repentance is the difference between acknowledging a gambling or pornography addiction and seeking counsel or help to begin recovery. Repentance is the difference between acknowledging the issue of gossip and deciding not to participate in, or even listen to, such conversations. Repentance requires action. If we truly want to have conversation with God we must first connect with Him, and we cannot truly connect without repentance.

2. Pray to align.

As believers, many of us use prayer as an opportunity to tell God all our thoughts, concerns, and most commonly, our desires, yet, we miss the opportunity to align with God through prayer. Tagging a prayer with "not my will but thy will" and/or "in Jesus' name" isn't necessarily going to result in alignment. Too often we expect things to happen simply because we asked and believed. Prayer doesn't work by the authority of our words but by the authority of God's word. This is why I believe that knowledge of God's word is fundamental for powerful prayer. Yes, it's true that He wants to grant us the desires of our heart, however, if we are truly aligned with God our greatest desire will be for continued alignment; our desire will directly reflect God's will for us.

Prayer and our prayer requests are personal and unique to each of us; prayer flows from our desire. As children of God, we can, and should, seek God for things such as promotion in our careers, fruitful ministries, and joyful marriages—whatever it is that is important to us. God wants us to live abundantly, He wants us to enjoy deep, meaningful relationships, good health, and, yes, even wealth. When we are careful to be within God's will for us, not only will He bless us with those things but also with so much more. However, asking God to bless a relationship and/or a household that enjoys the benefits of marriage without the commitment and confines of marriage is futile. It's futile to seek God for financial blessings without any plan to budget and practice good stewardship. Such prayers likely won't yield the desired result because prayer is only half the equation. If we are unwilling to do what is within our power to improve our situation, how then can we expect God to do it for us? While today's culture has made cohabitation and sex outside of marriage commonplace and acceptable, those of us who read God's word know that we should not be driven by lust (Thessalonians 4:3-5) and instead should only enjoy sex within the confines of marriage (1 Corinthians 7:2). Those of us who study God's word understand that He clearly expects us to be good stewards of all that He blesses us with, and if we desire more, we first have to be good stewards of what he has already given us. If we gamble our money away and miss our bills, why would God bless us with more money to gamble with? Poor financial stewardship will not lead to increase and may even result in a loss of current blessings (Matthew 25:14-30). Biblical finance expert Howard Dayton says the Bible references money or possessions 2,350 times. While I am not versed in the entirety of those scriptures, I know that God does tell us to budget and keep track of our money (Luke 14:28-30, Proverbs 27:23).

When we know God's word and understand His principles we can model our lives properly, repent, and then connect to Him. This is when prayer has unimaginable power. 1John 5:14 tells us that anything we ask according to His will He will hear, so, in other words, when we pray in line with God's word (and even remind Him of His word) He hears us— we have His attention. Furthermore, 1John 5:15 that tells us if He heard us, then we know that we have whatever we've asked. Praying within God's word also aligns us— our will with His will, and our heart with His heart. This alignment is what prompts God to move. Prayer should be a place of alignment otherwise it is futile.

3. Pray to hear

We live in a culture today where everyone is operating either on a meticulous schedule, or by routine, or flying by the seat of their pants from one thing to the next. With today's lifestyles it seems that setting aside time each day for study and prayer is a hard-earned win. Many believers have struggled for years to establish a regular routine of time dedicated to God. While I, as well as many other Christian leaders, often encourage believers to schedule time each day to spend with God, this advice (which has often gone unapplied) is frequently followed up with reading suggestions and a reminder to take time to pray. Many of us who have gotten into the habit of study and prayer know about how long to schedule for these activities. We quickly gain an idea of how long our reading will take and wind up praying prayers that are pretty consistent in length. There is nothing wrong with this. These consistent prayers usually include praise, repentance and request sealed in the name of Jesus. However, those of us who ask God to show us His will for us, or who seek His direction, often miss the opportunity to allow God to speak. God speaks not only through His written word but also directly to us, in spirit. John 10:27 says, "My sheep listen to my voice; I know them, and they follow me". Prayer is a time to connect, align, and have conversation with God. Prayer does not have to be a one sided conversation. God wants to speak to His people; He wants us to hear Him, to listen, and to recognize His voice. However, many of us fail to fully quiet ourselves during our prayer time.

It's not necessary to include quiet time *each* time we pray, however, we should be careful to include it in our prayer life. God wants to speak to us, and prayer is the perfect opportunity to allow Him to do so. When we pray, we've already created the space to communicate with God. Furthermore, we've repented and aligned ourselves with God so we are connected with Him; we just need to create the opportunity for Him to speak. Creating the opportunity for God to speak may sound simple but it may feel difficult to create. After we've connected and shared all of our thoughts and concerns with the Father, we need to learn to quiet our hearts and minds. I believe that this is a discipline that takes time to master.

Our environment also plays a big role in our ability to engage in conversation with God. On multiple occasions Christ separated himself to pray and connect with God the Father. If we want to deeply connect in prayer and hear from God, we should follow Christ's example. We should steal away from everyone else and from any distractions. The same principles that I outlined for creating our devotional environment are the same principles that we can utilize in creating a distraction free environment that is conducive to our hearing from God. The devil loves to use distraction to keep us from being all that we have been created to be, and we must guard against being easily distracted. We must be intentional and dedicated to connecting with, and hearing from, God. Once we are connected and our hearts and minds are clear, if we exercise some discipline to stay in that connected moment, God can, and often will, speak to us. Again, creating this space and opportunity requires discipline, and it is the part of prayer that we cannot plan for in terms of duration. When God speaks, He may speak only a few words or He may pour into us, keeping our attention for a while. Even though

He may not speak long it will always require or elicit a response from us. We may be prompted to enter back into prayer, we may be prompted to worship, or we may be prompted to praise.

Whenever God connects and speaks to us we want to experience Him in the fullness of that moment. So, maybe we generally take 20 minutes for prayer, but God's response doubled that— He knows all we need to accomplish each day, and how much time we need to accomplish it, and He will always provide us the means to do what HE desires for us to accomplish for the day. So often we rush God without thought because we have a schedule, but the sad truth is, that there is often time for TV, random conversations, or some sort of down time that could easily be made into productive time so that we can hear from God; it boils down to managing our priorities. Don't miss God speaking to you because you allow no room for Him in your schedule.

We pray to connect, align, and hear. Healthy relationships are based on healthy communication, so we need to be diligent in making sure that God can not only speak to us through His word, but that He can also speak directly to us. When we create the opportunity for God to speak during prayer He will. God will hear us and answer us; He will give us guidance and direction. Keeping that in mind, we must be careful to move in the direction that God leads and not simply in a direction that we feel is right. If there is any question as to whether or not God has spoken, we can always find confirmation in His word. Knowing God's word is knowing Him. Knowing Him means we know His character, and we can filter moral decisions based on who God is. For decisions based on direction, if we operate in the last clear direction we were given, God will make known what we need to know for the next steps at the appropriate time.

Rooted believers should not be scared of moving forward in assignment because we know that our steps are ordered (Psalms 37:23); the Holy Spirit dwells within us and will cause us to take the right path (1 Corinthians 3:16, Ezekiel 36:27, John 14:26, John 16:13). The more that we study, connect, align and allow space for God to speak, the more that we are pouring into our spirits and making the Holy Spirit a stronger, bigger influence in our lives. The more that we allow the Holy Spirit to lead, the more God can speak because we are being good stewards of the direction and vision He has given us. As the process of creating regular study habits is circular, so is the process of creating a strong prayer life.

Vision Check: In addition to having time set aside for study and prayer, do you allow adequate room for God to respond? If you do but aren't getting a response from God, are you taking the time to make sure you are aligned with God's word and fully repented so that you can truly connect without barrier?

Chapter Eight

Strengthen by Connection

As a pastor's wife, I find it frustrating to witness the ease with which some believers dismiss the importance of connecting with a local church. Although I understand many of the common misgivings about church, I also know that community amongst believers is a must. Yes, some people have been mistreated or even abused by individual churches, but those instances only prove that some churches, or the people making up those individual churches, are broken; those instances do not mitigate the fact that the spiritual community of a church is a vital lifeline for believers. Before I make the case for connecting to a church let me address the two most common excuses believers use in reference to lax church attendance.

1. "Church hurt"

   This tends to be the most popular reason why believers no long attend a particular church, or any church for that matter. Church hurt is any kind of offense that happens within the church, and because it happens within the church, then no matter what the offense, it often feels very personal. The reality is that in every church we may encounter unkind words and/or poor behavior. Every church is flawed because every church is made up of flawed people. These flaws cannot be escaped— we all (myself included) have been hurt by people we expected to love and/or lead us. However, if we have been authentic in our walk, then it's very likely that we have also been the source of "church hurt" for someone else. This is because we are all in relationship, we are all flawed, and we all have shortcomings. Church hurt happens; it happens when we aren't expecting it and sometimes when we are feeling the most vulnerable. While some church hurts are intentional, I've found over the years that most are unintentional.

Often, church hurt is the result of either the wrong delivery, the wrong timing, speaking with the wrong person or having the wrong friends. Unfortunately, though they may be unintentional, there isn't an easy fix for any of these hurts. With respect to delivery, the fact is that even in good relationships it is easy for one to sound uncaring when bringing a touchy subject to the table. When a sensitive subject is being addressed, it is also easy to miss the love being displayed in the fact that someone cared enough to broach the subject. It's hard to risk causing pain, especially when an otherwise good relationship is involved.

Hurt caused by bad timing is usually the result of a lack of understanding, or knowledge, of the mental and/or emotional well-being of the person being approached. The absence of such knowledge or understanding can easily make a small problem feel life changing. Bad timing can be "the straw that breaks the camel's back" when added to what is already a heavy load.

When hurt stems from a message being delivered by the wrong person, then there is, very plainly, either a lack of proper relationship, or a lack of understanding of the state of the relationship by the deliverer. Dealing with church hurt and having the wrong friends has more to do with the aftermath of the hurt than the initial situation itself. When someone's actions cause emotional discomfort, whether intentional or unintentional, the natural response is to look for comfort elsewhere, however, few people seek God first for this comfort. Usually our peers are who we turn to first for comfort, and sadly their thoughts and opinions often carry the most weight. When we do this, we are prioritizing our friend's thoughts and opinions over God's, and thus, we are allowing them to influence the lens through which we view the situation. Seeking Godly counsel is advisable in almost any situation, but when it comes to church hurt, it is important for us to remember that we can count on one of two responses. On one hand, our mature peers will seek to comfort, encourage, and provide impartial insight. On the other hand, those who only seek to be "good" friends, are less mature in their walk, or have a similar grudge (against the deliverer), will seek strategically to deepen the hurt, or validate our pain in a way that unknowingly makes us angry.

Ultimately, many church hurts are, at the root, accidental, and they are often aggravated because they touch on areas that are already a source of guilt, or conviction. Because many of us aren't ready to deal with conviction, many church hurts are received and handled just as poorly as they are delivered. Instead of seeking comfort and affirmation from our friends, we should seek God and allow Him to either affirm or convict us. Seeking God is particularly important because sometimes the cause of our hurt isn't that our shortcomings were pointed out, but rather, that what was said was true, and we aren't ready to deal with it. We have all been hurt, and we have all hurt. We must learn to extend grace to those who have hurt us and likewise, when possible, seek forgiveness from those whom we have hurt. After all, forgiveness is at the heart of who God is.

2. Myth: "We (all believers) are the church, so attending a church is not necessary"

   The Bible clearly teaches of two different types of church, the first being the "Universal Church" which, indeed, is inclusive of all believers regardless of location or denomination.

   For we were all baptized by one Spirit so as to form one body—whether Jews or Gentiles, slave or free—and we were all given the one Spirit to drink.

   1 Corinthians 12:13 (NIV)

   ***

   Now I rejoice in what I am suffering for you, and I fill up in my flesh what is still lacking in regard to Christ's afflictions, for the sake of his body, which is the church

   Colossians 1:24 (NIV)

It is absolutely true that every person in submission to God, with the indwelling of the Holy Spirit, is part of the body of Christ, which is

129

the church—the "Universal Church". But, the Bible also clearly teaches us that we are to assemble, and the Universal Church—the entire body of Christ—will not be assembled or gathered together until the rapture.

The second church referenced in the Bible is the "Local Church". The Local Church is a manifestation of the Universal Church. We are called to be believers together, not simply as individuals (1Corntithians 1:2). Hebrews 10:25 reminds us that we should *"not [be] giving up meeting together, as some are in the habit of doing..."*. This scripture suggests that, the coming together of believers has always been a topic of discussion and so, clear direction has been given. The presence of the Local Church is shown in the New Testament. Paul writes letters to the churches at Ephesus and Corinth as well as many others. Additionally, larger areas, like Galatia, are described as having multiple churches. These local churches were the result of members of the larger Body of Christ coming together.

There are many lessons found in New Testament scripture that teach the importance, even the necessity, of the Local Church for encouragement, growth, and the ability to care for God's people.

The overall goal of every Christ-centered church is to bring God glory. Churches do this through the development of their people. Every Christian should be following the example of Paul by continuing to "press toward the goal, the high calling of God". We should be ever evolving, growing and maturing. We are created as communal beings and Acts 2:42 models for us the fact that the assembling of believers is where we find a community that is after God's heart.

They devoted themselves to the apostles' teaching and to fellowship, to the breaking of bread and to prayer.

Acts 2:42 (NIV)

To be clear, while streaming church services, spirit-led podcasts, Bible study, and coffee with peers may be edifying to our spirits, this isn't the picture, painted throughout the Bible, of the Local Church. A local church does more personal work; it targets teachings and activities to the body of believers that attend. Additionally, it reflects God in the community by serving the needs of the community while evangelizing to the community. Most of the activities that I mentioned before (streaming services, podcasts etc.) primarily serve those who are already saved. While such activities are wonderful, they do not necessarily challenge us or hold us accountable to the same extent that a local church can.

Healthy local churches are diverse, or actively growing more diverse, in age, ethnicity, and socioeconomic standing. The Great Commission instructs us to make disciples of every nation. Ephesians 4:11 says that God Himself appoints people to instruct and teach us— those people take the form of preachers, Bible study and Sunday school teachers, elders, etc. within local churches. Those who do such work should be as diverse as the work itself is. The work of the church, in our personal lives, is to encourage, equip, and then challenge us in ways that cause us to live lives that reflect God. Our lifestyles will then dictate our reputations, and with those reputations, we are able to disciple others and build up the body of Christ. This is the job of every believer.

In light of its evangelistic mission, the church is a vital part of all communities. Local churches have to opportunity to be powerhouses within their communities. This is part of the reason why some places of worship around the world are regulated by government and are targets of terrorist groups. The mere presence of a church can spark hope and change in any community. Churches are regarded as the House of God, as places of refuge, and as places of resource. We see this regard reflected after national tragedies as people run to churches for comfort, safety, and help with basic needs. The need for holistic ministry cannot be met by television, live stream, or by podcast. These needs must be met by the Local Church. They must be met by us. God gifted us all uniquely, and so our presence and our participation within our local churches are vital to carry out this work. Collectively, we can meet the needs of our communities.

⁴ For just as each of us has one body with many members, and these members do not all have the same function, ⁵ so in Christ we, though many, form one body, and each member belongs to all the others. ⁶ We have different gifts, according to the grace given to each of us. If your gift is prophesying, then prophesy in accordance with your faith; ⁷ if it is serving, then serve; if it is teaching, then teach; ⁸ if it is to encourage, then give encouragement; if it is giving, then give generously; if it is to lead, do it diligently; if it is to show mercy, do it cheerfully.

Romans 12:4-8 (NIV)

In Ephesians 4:16 (NIV), Paul explains " *From him the whole body, joined and held together by every supporting ligament, grows and builds itself up in love, as each part does its work.*" This is yet another reason why each of us is pivotal to the success of the church. As individual believers are encouraged in, and equipped for, service, church becomes the place where love blossoms. Church is the place where vision for our communities should be inspired. I believe that God desires the church to be a place of distribution. Blessing our communities with the blessings God has so abundantly poured into each of us— whether it be money, kind words, or working hands— is the best way to distribute the love of God. Sharing the love of God is how we begin the work of discipleship, which is the mandate of every believer. The Local Church is integral to properly equipping us to do work greater than ourselves. The Local Church does vital work— work that works for our good, benefits those around us and gives God great glory.

"You are the light of the world. A town built on a hill cannot be hidden."

Matthew 5:14(NIV)

Vision Check: If the Bible teaches the importance of the local church for the believer as well as for the community, is it not the job of each believer to build the local church up? God instructs not only on the importance of church attendance, but also on the importance of the work of the church. Do you know your spiritual gifts? Are you using your gifts and talents to advance the mission of the church?

Chapter Nine

Strength for the Body of Christ

Yes, we go to church to worship God, and hopefully, to be an active part of a ministry and a vision greater than ourselves, however, we innately go to be in relationship. God designed us not to just be in relationship with Him, but also with others. In fact, our relationship with God should teach us how to have healthy relationships with others (but that's another book!).

Despite the often-repeated claim, "I don't care how people feel about me, or what they think about me", in some respect we, as human beings, do care, and as believers, we must care. It's always much more comfortable to be well liked than talked about poorly, to be invited rather than left out, to receive compliments rather than criticism. Whether or not we openly admit it, words and unkind behavior DO cause hurt. I'm not suggesting that everyone should or will like us, but I am suggesting that we all do and should care, on some level. Believers should especially be careful about dismissing care and concern in regard to how people view us. First, we are supposed to be representatives of Christ, and I can't recall a single instance where He responded to ANYONE in such a fashion. Second, we are supposed to disciple others and bring them to Christ; how can we lead when we don't care? Third, and most importantly, the Bible ranks relationship (first with God and second with others) as the most important aspect of life.

[36] "Teacher, which is the greatest commandment in the Law?"

[37] Jesus replied: "'Love the Lord your God with all your heart and with all your soul and with all your mind.' [38] This is the first and greatest commandment. [39] And the second is like it: 'Love your neighbor as yourself.' [40] All the Law and the Prophets hang on these two commandments."

Matthew 22:36-40 NIV

Thus, caring about relationships within the body of Christ, and with the people with whom we come into contact, is not only essential, it is a commandment.

Many of us, who regularly attend church and work in ministry in some capacity, are well intentioned and have a deep desire to be in right relationship with God and His people. We understand that church is vital to us, that the work to be done is both crucial to our communities and mandated by God. Yet, we often find ourselves overwhelmed by accusations of hypocrisy from people outside of the church and subject to shame by people inside of the church. If we are not strong, this negativity can hinder our confidence in the work we have called to do. Self-doubt and lack of self-confidence are greatly influenced by today's culture and are steadily seeping into the hearts and minds of believers. A lack of self-confidence and self-worth is something that I regularly see within the church body, and it doesn't seem to matter the gender or age of the individual; although the outward expression of these feelings may be different across different demographics, the issue is the same. It can be seen in the hesitant voice of a gifted singer, in the lack of desire to try ministry in a new way, in the doubtfulness of one's ability to pray, or in the lack of authority over the things God has granted victory over. Fortunately, this lack of self-worth or self-confidence eases as we mature in Christ because we develop our confidence in Him (2 Corinthians 3:1-6), and in His calling upon us. Still, what others think of us will, on occasion, cause moments of doubt.

Although struggles with self-confidence and self-worth are internal for the most part, we can still greatly influence other believers, for good or for bad, in these areas. It is for this reason that God instructs us on how we should treat each other. We are commanded to love one another in word and deed (John 13:34). Loving one another is not always easy and sometimes we have to grow in it. Thank God for grace that allows us to grow into His love, and our ability to allow that love to flow from us. The growing process, while messy, does not excuse us from knowing and striving to behave in a way that reflects God's love and instruction. We cannot allow ourselves to be complacent in our messiness. Instead, we must decide that in spite of mistakes we will strive to show God's love. Loving someone well doesn't mean that we are always going to be able to do the nice or easy things, sometimes it means we have to do the hard things. Ephesians 4:32 says that we must extend forgiveness to others, and Colossians 3:16 reminds us that we must let the word of Christ dwell within us that we might teach and admonish each other with wisdom. Forgiveness is a hard, internal battle to win. To teach and admonish others not only requires a hard, internal battle, it also requires a hard, external conversation. Teaching and admonishment, for those of us who are in positions of leadership within our churches, are especially difficult tasks. For those of us with friends outside of the will of God, these conversations are difficult tasks and can be extremely personal. Often, this is because we find these difficult conversations have to happen with people in whom we are invested and for whom we care deeply. Yet, we must keep in mind that we are in relationship not just to enjoy each other, but also to instruct each other in the word of God (Romans 15:14) and to spur each other in the right direction. Having strong relationships that reflect this principle is foundational for building a strong church body. If we truly love someone, we will not stand idly by and watch them travel farther along the wrong road.

Loving someone is helping them live well and within God's design for His people.

As we learned in the chapter on forgiveness loving others also means we need to speak well of them. Speaking well of others isn't just important when it comes to forgiveness; it is important in every aspect of relationship. Unfortunately, it is common for believers to participate in gossip, both by listening to it and by repeating it. Believers will often hide either behind the excuse: "I'm just telling the truth" or behind feigned concern. The truth is that there is seldom any reason to repeat gossip unless some action is required. Discussing a circumstance or a situation that we are concerned about, and believe to be true, should prompt action. Action can be seeking resources to provide for a need, seeking counsel from leadership on behalf of those involved in the situation, or seeking God in prayer. As I pointed out earlier, if you aren't standing in the gap, you are probably standing in judgement. If we are not moved to help or right a situation, then we are likely gossiping. We should speak well of others, bless others, and honor others.

Romans 12:10 says that we should be devoted to one another in love, honoring one another above ourselves. In order to authentically honor others, we must have the right attitude. Honor comes from a heart of love causing us to care for others before ourselves; this authentic honor also requires a humble heart. It is impossible to really honor someone when we are feeling slighted and believe some acknowledgement is due to us. It is hard to honor others when we feel better than them in some way. Romans 12:3 and Philippians 2:3 warn us to guard against thinking and esteeming ourselves either more highly than we ought or above others.

Love not only causes us to bless and honor others, it also compels us to be in service of others. Galatians 5:13 reminds us to serve one another humbly in love. How we love and serve others is a reflection of how we love and serve God. Believers should always bear in mind Matthew 25:40; "*The King will reply, 'Truly I tell you, whatever you did for one of the least of these brothers and sisters of mine, you did for me.'*". Teaching, correcting, speaking well of, standing in the gap for, and showing honor to others are all ways in which we should be serving each other and causing love to abound— in the lives of God's people, in our churches and in our communities. The abundance of love and honor are the manifestation of a strong body of believers. Love that results in honor will allow us to treat each other better, to work together better, and to honor God better together.

Imitating Christ's Humility

2 Therefore if you have any encouragement from being united with Christ, if any comfort from his love, if any common sharing in the Spirit, if any tenderness and compassion, [2] then make my joy complete by being like-minded, having the same love, being one in spirit and of one mind. [3] Do nothing out of selfish ambition or vain conceit. Rather, in humility value others above yourselves, [4] not looking to your own interests but each of you to the interests of the others.

[5] In your relationships with one another, have the same mindset as Christ Jesus:

[6] Who, being in very nature God, did not consider equality with God something to be

used to his own advantage;
⁷ rather, he made himself nothing
by taking the very nature of a servant,
being made in human likeness.
⁸ And being found in appearance as a man,
he humbled himself
by becoming obedient to death—
even death on a cross!

⁹ Therefore God exalted him to the highest
place
and gave him the name that is above every name,
¹⁰ that at the name of Jesus every knee should bow,
in heaven and on earth and under the earth,
¹¹ and every tongue acknowledge that Jesus Christ is
Lord,
to the glory of God the Father.

¹² Therefore, my dear friends, as you have
always obeyed—not only in my presence, but now
much more in my absence—continue to work out your
salvation with fear and trembling, ¹³ for it is God who
works in you to will and to act in order to fulfill his
good purpose.

¹⁴ Do everything without grumbling or arguing,
¹⁵ so that you may become blameless and pure,
"children of God without fault in a warped and crooked
generation." Then you will shine among them like
stars in the sky¹⁶⁽ᵃ⁾ as you hold firmly to the word of
life.

Philippians 2:1-16

Vision Check: Is the love of Christ reflected in your
relationships? Based on how you serve others are you
serving God well? Do you strengthen those around
you with the honor God mandates? Is your service
strong, and to the best of your ability, according to
how God has gifted you, and done as unto Him rather
than people?

Part Three

Building a Strong Body

Dear friend, I pray that you may enjoy good health and that all may go well with you, even as your soul is getting along well.

3 John 1:2(NIV)

Chapter Ten

The Bible and the Body of a Believer

Just as God expects us to be good stewards of our ministries, finances, and relationships, He also expects us to be good stewards of our health. Too often, we diligently strive for better marriages, nice homes, and fully funded savings accounts, but we don't strive for good health in the same manner. It has become pretty well known that everyone, believers and non-believers alike, is growing less healthy. We know that we should eat better foods, practice portion control, and exercise. Despite having been told by our doctors that we need to change for our health, we often continue along the same paths while making minimal, if any, changes. People dealing with heart disease, high cholesterol, high blood pressure, or diabetes overwhelmingly opt for taking prescription medications rather than implementing lifestyle changes. Yet, the fact is that individuals tend to overestimate the benefits of medicine and grossly underestimate the effects and benefits of lifestyle change. For example, research has shown that 90 percent of heart disease is completely preventable with significant and intentional lifestyle adjustments. Likewise, studies have shown that Type 2 diabetes is better treated, and even eradicated, through proper diet and exercise than by management through medicine; the same is true for hypertension. While the medicinal management of diseases is sometimes necessary, it rarely allows us to enjoy fully the physical bodies and all of the physical capabilities that God initially designed us to have.

Although many churches work to address the spiritual and physical needs of their members and communities, this is one area that is easily overlooked. Many churches do a great job building up our spiritual needs and teaching us how to practically apply God's word to our everyday lives, however, after spending more than half of my life actually paying attention during services and studies, I've noticed that God's concern for our physical health is rarely taught. Most times, when our physical bodies are brought up it is in reference to abstaining from smoking, pre-marital sex, drugs, or alcohol. On the rare occasion when topics like diabetes, heart health, and the importance of exercise are discussed, the discussion is often forgotten by the time of the next fellowship meal (complete with artery clogging main dishes and sugar-filled desserts). To be clear, it would be fine for the church to host indulgent meals if the church also taught the importance of good health from the standpoint of God's word. The thing is, as the general population becomes less healthy, so does the church; believers have fallen into the trap of accepting, and in some cases even encouraging, unhealthy habits or lifestyles. It's troubling that until we are seeking God for victory over illness, or for recovery of some sort, we overlook the fact that God cares very deeply about our physical health.

When God designed us, He took special care and intricately designed even our physical bodies. He meant for our bodies to serve us well, to serve Him well, and to serve as a temple for the Holy Spirit.

[19] Do you not know that your bodies are temples of the Holy Spirit, who is in you, whom you have received from God? You are not your own; [20] you were bought at a price. Therefore honor God with your bodies.

1 Corinthians 6:19-20 (NIV)

This scripture should serve as reminder of 3 things:

1. Our bodies are the temple of the Holy Spirit, and just as we should have reverence for the House of God we should have reverence for our bodies, because He dwells in both.

2. Jesus died so that we might have life and live an abundant life. Enjoying the abundance of God's blessings is impossible if life is a struggle due to poor health.

3. We are to honor God with our bodies. Honoring God with our bodies is not about merely abstaining from sexual immorality and drugs; honoring God with our bodies is about taking great care of them— ensuring that they are the best they can possibly be.

1 Corinthians 3:17 says *"If anyone destroys God's temple, God will destroy that person; for God's temple is sacred, and you together are that temple".* Each of our individual bodies is a temple for the Holy Spirit,

and together, our collective bodies make up God's temple. God is warning us in this scripture that He will destroy those who destroy His temple. With each day, the signs that we are destroying the temple are more and more prevalent; these signs have names like Fatty Liver Disease, Heart Disease, Type 2 Diabetes, Gallbladder Disease, High Blood Pressure, and High Cholesterol. Praise God for His loving grace and bountiful mercy that He continues to pour on all of us despite our destructive behavior. Some cancers, arthritis, and breathing and sleep disorders, are also signs of destruction. While our health is not a salvation issue, it IS a stewardship issue and it DOES matter to God. 2 Peter 1:3 reminds us that God "has given us everything we need for a godly life". When it comes to our health there is no exception. The Bible makes plain the tie between our mental, spiritual and physical health.

7 Do not be wise in your own eyes;
fear the Lord and shun evil.
8 This will bring health to your body
and nourishment to your bones.

Proverbs 3:7-8(NIV)

151

***

Dear friend, I pray that you may enjoy good health and that all may go well with you, even as your soul is getting along well

3 John 1:2(NIV)

***

A heart at peace gives life to the body,

but envy rots the bones.

Proverbs 14:30(NIV)

***

Gracious words are a honeycomb,

sweet to the soul and healing to the bones

Proverbs 16:24(NIV)

***

A cheerful heart is good medicine,

but a crushed spirit dries up the bones.

Proverbs 17:22(NIV)

Science has begun exploring the link between mental and physical health, and it is just beginning to explore the link between spiritual health and physical health. Yet, God has known from the beginning that mental health, spiritual health, and physical health are all inextricably connected. As a result, I believe that this is an area in which believers should be leading. Realizing that our physical health is important to God, we can begin to make our own changes and then begin to inspire change within those around us. Yet, knowing and understanding God's will for our health and body is only part of the work; we must also be able to lead by example. 1 Corinthians 9:26, in the Amplified Bible Version, relays this message perfectly, "*But [like a boxer] I strictly discipline my body and make it my slave, so that, after I have preached [the gospel] to others, I myself will not somehow be disqualified [as unfit for service]."*

Chapter Eleven

Size vs. Strength

Where the question of health is concerned, popular culture has seemingly decided that size is the number one indicator of whether or not a person is healthy. The problem with using size as an indicator of health is that it is extremely subjective— according to where we live and the culture of our community. I experience this first hand as I have several different communities in which I spend my time.

My personal communities though diverse, are predominately People of Color, they view me as thin— even too thin. Several times I have been cautioned not to lose any more weight, and I have often received comments along the lines of "every time I see you you're skinnier". I can never decide if such comments come from places of shade, envy, or legitimate concern. In my experience, if you are perceived as thin, anyone and everyone feels as if it's okay to comment on, or give advice about, your body. My weight, like most, fluctuates. Most times I am the size that I want to be. However, there are other times where I am either above or beneath the target that I've set for myself. Sometimes I'm fluffier as a result of having more down time and/or eating more processed foods; sometimes I'm leaner as a result of working more and/or being careful to fuel my body properly in order to maintain my optimal performance level. Being from a community that loves thick women and celebrates curves, the same people who comment about my size are far less likely to tell someone else that they ought to be careful about gaining any weight or make any comment about their body.

In comparison, my professional communities, across several gyms that are diverse but predominantly Caucasian, have given me the reputation of being larger than most of the group fitness instructors, but fitting the physique and look of a trainer— this is in spite of the fact that I fill both roles. It caught me off guard the first time I overheard one class member say to another "Don't be fooled because she is big— she'll kick your butt." I was further surprised when I was told that I fit the trainer role better because I'm thick and more muscular.

Although I am the same size throughout the course of the day and throughout my communities, they each view me very differently based upon their own culture and beliefs. I love both communities and believe that I am loved within both communities. The reason I point out the (uncomfortable) difference between the two is to highlight, in part, why it is futile to allow any culture or community influence what size we should be. We all move through various communities during the course of a day or week, and no two communities are alike; yet, too often, we allow community and culture to shape what we think about ourselves and each other.

Overwhelmingly, most cultures have deemed big as bad and small, or thin, as good; however, those categories are very broad and usually do not reflect the physiological makeup of a person's body. Yes, if our doctor diagnoses us as either obese or morbidly obese, we are likely large and hence our largeness is not good due the negative effects on our organs and mobility. It is also true that if our doctor diagnoses us as either underweight, or emaciated, we are likely small and hence our smallness is not good because of the effect on our organs. Although size can be a good indicator of health, it is not the best indicator and that, in part, is why I believe we should focus on size a little less. The other reason I believe that we should focus less on size is because I don't believe size matters much to God as long as we are healthy.

Nowhere in the Bible does God deem health good or bad based purely on size. What the Bible does differentiate between is good health and poor health, healthy and unhealthy. When considering whether we are healthy or unhealthy, we should take account of our overall health including, but not using exclusively, our size. The reality is that someone who is small, or healthy looking, can be just as unhealthy or sick as someone twice their size. Likewise, someone who is forty pounds heavier than the doctor thinks they should be can be twice as healthy someone half their size. God has divinely designed each of us to be unique, and we are fearfully and wonderfully made (Psalm 139:14). There is no one size fits all when it comes to our health; God isn't concerned about whether we are a size four or fourteen. Instead, He cares that we honor Him with our bodies, that we are in good health, and that we are strong. He desires for us to be: of a sound or strong mind, strong in spirit, and strong in body.

Throughout His written word, God admonishes us to be strong. God doesn't mean for us to be strong in only one area of our lives, but He asks us to be strong in every area of our lives. When God specifically means to speak to one aspect of our being He does so. For example, when strength is intended to refer to spirit only, it is clearly stated, as in Ephesians 3:1, "*I pray that out of his glorious riches he may strengthen you with power through his Spirit in your inner being*". God is careful to talk explicitly about our mindsets; He is careful to talk explicitly about our spirits, and He is just as careful to talk specifically about our physical bodies as well. Having spent an exhaustive amount of time researching this particular topic, I'm unable to find any instance in scripture where size is of concern to God. Nowhere in the Bible could I find reference to or correlations between size and health; and I believe that if God was concerned with our body measurements, He would have included some guidelines. What God does include in His written word, however, are scriptures that apply to both our physical strength, and spiritual strength. Allow me to walk through a few particularly noteworthy examples.

In Isaiah 40:29, the prophet writes of God,

He gives strength to the weary

and increases the power of the weak.

I'd break this scripture down like this: He gives strength to those of us who are tired and will increase the strength of those who are too weak for our purpose. This may be an increase of physical strength to preach His word, spiritual strength to encourage ourselves or mental strength in order to avoid temptation. Another noteworthy passage is found in Mark12:30.

Love the Lord your God with all your heart and with all your soul and with all your mind and with all your strength.

In other words, we should love the Lord with all of our hearts, with complete sincerity. We should love Him with all of our spirit by being filled with the Holy Spirit.

We should love Him with all of our minds, or intellect, and we should love Him with all of our strength, or energies, in word and action.

God's concern with strength is not only addressed in philosophical or observational statements, it is also addressed in narrative illustrations in the Bible. When recalling Bible stories of physical strength, most of us would gravitate toward the story of Samson; however, for my purpose I'd like to bring our attention to "The Proverbs 31 Woman".

The Wife of Noble Character

[10] A wife of noble character who can find?
She is worth far more than rubies.
[11] Her husband has full confidence in her
and lacks nothing of value.
[12] She brings him good, not harm,
all the days of her life.
[13] She selects wool and flax
and works with eager hands.
[14] She is like the merchant ships,
bringing her food from afar.

¹⁵ She gets up while it is still night;
   she provides food for her family
   and portions for her female servants.
¹⁶ She considers a field and buys it;
   out of her earnings she plants a vineyard.
¹⁷ She sets about her work vigorously;
   her arms are strong for her tasks.
¹⁸ She sees that her trading is profitable,
   and her lamp does not go out at night.
¹⁹ In her hand she holds the distaff
   and grasps the spindle with her fingers.
²⁰ She opens her arms to the poor
   and extends her hands to the needy.
²¹ When it snows, she has no fear for her household;
   for all of them are clothed in scarlet.
²² She makes coverings for her bed;
   she is clothed in fine linen and purple.
²³ Her husband is respected at the city gate,
   where he takes his seat among the elders of the
                        land.
²⁴ She makes linen garments and sells them,
   and supplies the merchants with sashes.
²⁵ She is clothed with strength and dignity;
   she can laugh at the days to come.

²⁶ She speaks with wisdom,
and faithful instruction is on her tongue.
²⁷ She watches over the affairs of her household
and does not eat the bread of idleness.
²⁸ Her children arise and call her blessed;
her husband also, and he praises her:
²⁹ "Many women do noble things,
but you surpass them all."
³⁰ Charm is deceptive, and beauty is fleeting;
but a woman who fears the Lord is to be praised.
³¹ Honor her for all that her hands have done,
and let her works bring her praise at the city gate.

Proverbs 31:10-31

All too often this scripture is brushed aside until it is taught at a women's event or on Mother's Day. It is interesting how, by and large, men and women alike have earmarked this scripture as one of very few scriptures that, seemingly, only applies to one gender when, in fact, all of scripture belongs to all of us. Galatians 3:28 says "*There is neither Jew nor Gentile, neither slave nor free, nor is there male and female, for you are all one in Christ Jesus.*" Every believer can follow many of the examples set by this industrious woman. When looking specifically to physical strength we can all look to the proverbs 31 woman.

Even though I referenced this particular passage of scripture to talk about physical strength, let's take a moment to appreciate all the strengths the Proverbs 31 woman models for us. I love how this particular passage begins with a statement that this woman is essentially invaluable before going on to describe her day-to-day activities. At all times, this woman brings value and goodness to her home and is trust-worthy. The scripture says that she works with eager hands, and not only does she work with purpose, it goes on to say she does so intelligently. The Proverbs 31 woman creates balance in her life, making sure that she can be productive at her work while also caring for her home and family. She is financially savvy, considering her financial situation before purchasing land. So, she must be organized and budget. This passage ultimately teaches us that because The Proverbs 31 Woman does her part so diligently, her family is blessed and respected. She has no worry for the future; rather she will laugh and be joyful.

Let us not miss the fact that The Proverbs 31 Woman is blessed, and is a blessing, because of the work she is able to accomplish. We should note as well, that this passage is not just about "women's work"; it sets a wonderful example of what every believer should strive for— to be thought well of, to be trusted and to be a blessing to those to whom we are connected. The Proverbs 31 Woman demonstrates all of the types of strength that are discussed in this book. She is strong in mind; she handles business affairs. She is strong in spirit; she speaks wisdom and faithful instruction. Finally, she is strong in body; she can accomplish all the work before her. Yes, The Proverbs 31 Woman is also physically strong, and we should not miss the fact that her strength is specifically mentioned. Verses 17 and 31 work wonderfully together: *"She sets about her work vigorously; her arms are strong for her tasks.", " Honor her for all that her hands have done, and let her works bring her praise at the city gate."*. She is strong in mind, sprit, and body, and the result received is honor and praise for all the work she accomplishes.

We don't need to be Samson strong, but we do need enough physical strength to do the work that we are called to do in our homes, in our careers, and in our ministries. We need to follow the model of the Proverbs 31Woman; we must be strong enough to work vigorously. We must have both the physical strength and the stamina to complete our tasks with excellence. We cannot be content with just being the bare minimum, for if we have just a minimal amount of strength, we can count on minimal results, and we can be sure that we will not be entrusted with more. We must be careful about accepting the minimum and being complacent— complacency will never lead to more or greater and will often lead to less or even death. Let us take note that after all the description given within this one passage, not once is size mentioned, because it doesn't matter, it's not a marker of value or the ability to be great. Strength of mind, spirit, and body are all well covered here, and they are what allows the blessings to flow freely and joy to be present. The Proverbs 31 woman was indeed strong in mind and spirit, AND she was also strong in body.

Now that I've made the scriptural case for valuing strength over size, let's turn our attention to the science behind my position of valuing strength over size. Multiple studies have shown that it is not uncommon to be thin and metabolically unhealthy, and it's not as uncommon as we think to be overweight and metabolically fit. A meta-analysis of 51 different studies, led by Dr. Joel Ray, has shown that individuals who are under-weight have just as high a mortality rate as those who are over-weight. Furthermore, people whose weight and size are described as normal, but who have a high ratio of fat to lean body mass are at high risk to develop Type Two Diabetes, proving again that "normal" is not always healthy. Additionally, according to a study published in the Journal of the American Medical Association, those individuals within their ideal weight range (or under) with Type Two Diabetes have a higher risk of dying due to Type Two Diabetes. Another study published by this same journal found that while a BMI of 18.5 -24.9 is considered ideal, people with a Body Mass Index (BMI) of 25 to 30 had a lower risk of dying although they were considered overweight.

BMI ratios have been used for many years as an assessment for physical health, however, recent studies have begun to show that they are not accurate enough to assess an individual's health. A 2014 study conducted on people within the normal BMI range (15.5-24.9) showed that those people had a higher risk of metabolic concerns than any other group. Now, before those of us with BMIs higher than 24.9 get too happy, the point that I'm making is not that bigger is better or that small is bad. The point is that, when we combine all the various studies, we can conclude that size is not the best indicator of our physical health.

BMI is based on two measurements—weight and height. A BMI measurement says absolutely nothing about body composition and, in my opinion, is a terrible marker of health. When I regularly track my weight and combine that information with measurements other than height, I'm left with usable data that enables me to mark progress of the difference between fat or muscle loss and gain. In contrast, BMI doesn't detail the composition of a body; moreover, it doesn't indicate where the weight is held, and that information matters immensely (regardless of body size) since weight carried predominately around the midsection has been proven to be a cause for concern for heart health. In addition to providing no details pertaining to body composition, BMI measurements also don't distinguish between fat and muscle. For example, athletes often have BMI's that would categorize them as obese, but from simply looking at such people it would be clear that they are muscular, rather than overweight. Ultimately, BMI measurements are most useful for doctors who are determining a treatment course when hypertension or high cholesterol, or another aliment is present; outside of these situations, it is of little service.

Clearly size is not an accurate indicator of health. Nonetheless, we must be clear; carrying extra weight does increase our risk of poor health. The same is true of being underweight, and science is steadily proving that being at an "ideal weight" is no longer enough to ensure good health.

The ratio of lean mass (which includes skeleton, organs, muscle and their necessary counter parts, such as water) to our body mass, or fat, is crucial to determining our health. Independent of gender, age, or level of obesity, lean body mass has been shown to be a determining factor in cardiorespiratory fitness. The indication is that having more lean body mass increases good cardiorespiratory fitness thusly, improving heart health. Studies have also shown a direct link between increasing lean body mass and both the effects of diabetes and the ability to ward off diabetes. In fact, that particular research concludes "increases in muscle mass above even average levels were associated with additional protection against insulin resistance and prediabetes." [1]

From looking at the scientific research, it would seem that the best way to improve physically and live healthily is to focus more on strengthening our bodies. We can't do much to increase our skeletons (beyond increasing bone density), but we can increase our lean body mass by building muscle. We build muscle by exercising it consistently and by strategically applying pressure to it. This requires both cardiorespiratory training and strength training.

[1] *Srikanthan P, et al "Relative muscle mass is inversely associated with insulin resistance and prediabetes: Findings from the third NHANES" J Clin Endocrinol Metab 2011; DOI: 10.1210/jc.2011-0435.*

It is prudent for us to keep this mind as we deal with current health concerns and as we look toward the future.

As years pass, increasing our muscle and heart strength shifts beyond being important and becomes vital. People, even those of us who exercise regularly, begin to sit more and exercise less, the older we grow. This is dangerous because aging naturally causes muscle deterioration and muscle, at any age, is a "use it or lose it" commodity. The same is true for bone density. Our bodies regenerate our skeletons about every twelve years, and the good news is in this case is that form follows function. As we advance in years, our wisdom and commitment to our values should as well; we should begin to understand, more fully, who we are and God's plan for our lives. This maturation process will often spark a desire to be and/or do more. That desire may be to enjoy family and life more, to travel, to try a new career, or to be more active in ministry. No matter what the desire is, we are bound to need healthy bodies to fully accomplish it. Regularly participating in resistance and weight training will cause our skeleton to grow strong. While it won't ever be as strong as it was at age 20, it will be considerably stronger with training than it would be without training.

The good news is we don't have to do separate exercises to increase our muscle mass and bone density. The same exercises that increase muscle mass will work to increase bone density; the best way to accomplish this increase is through weight lifting. When done right, weight lifting increases muscle and applies pressure to the skeleton causing it create denser bones as it regenerates. Yes, this is work, but this work will ensure our ability to enjoy working in ministry, being with our families, and blessing those around us for years to come.

Strength is essential at every stage in life and even more so as we strive to slow the deterioration of the physical bodies with which we are to honor God. As we age, being small, but not strong, will transform into being frail and more susceptible to fractures and falls; while being big, but not strong, will transform into difficult to carry baggage and body aches. Both of these options will lead to a decrease in mobility, independence, and lifespan while we should be still enjoying the fruit from our labor earlier in life. However, if we are strong, by means of strength training, we will enjoy longer lives with independence and mobility.

Just as musculo-skeletal strength is critical to aging well heart health is also critical. Cardiovascular disease is leading cause of death in men and women across the United States including believers; in most cases cardiovascular disease is preventable. As we age, our heart's ability to effectively pump oxygen slowly diminishes; in order to combat this, we must exercise our hearts as we do our bodies. Strengthening our hearts is done through cardiorespiratory work (or as it is more commonly referred to, cardio/aerobic exercise). Regular cardio can reduce not only our blood pressure, but also our resting heart rate. This means that our hearts don't have to work quite as hard in our day to day lives. We should be fighting against allowing ourselves to fall "victim" to a disease that we scientifically have power over and that we can overcome through the power of God.

Honoring God with our bodies is about gaining and maintaining the best possible health for our individual bodies. It's about being fit for the work of God that is assigned to us— within our families, peer groups, churches, and communities. Just as each of our assignments is different and unique so are our bodies. We are built wonderfully matched to our assignments and given all we need to accomplish the work before us, if only we are good stewards of all our blessings (including our bodies). There is no one size fits all philosophy with God's calling and blessings. Therefore, there should be no one size fits all approach to health within the body of believers. Our bodies are as individualized as our personalities and our assignments are. God meant for us to be individual and our bodies are representative of that as well. God does not specify or prescribe a certain size for His people and, though it tries, it seems that even science cannot make the case for being a particular size. But, what God and science both agree on is the need for strong bodies. Culture often is the driving force behind determining the appropriate size, and our desire to be a certain size does not have to be a bad thing, it just needs to be in balance with what is necessary for a great life. There is nothing wrong with desiring a certain physique but, keep it in the right perspective; a strong body fit for work and life should be your focus, not size alone. The best size for you is the size that you feel comfortable being and that allows you to lead a long healthy life, glorifying God.

Chapter Twelve

Weight Loss Fads and Trendy Diet Plans

Although I firmly believe that strength is more important than size, size cannot be dismissed entirely. Aside from our personal physique preferences, there are some cases when size or weight does matter. Weight, and the composition of that weight (whether it's muscle or adipose tissue) matters most often when we are carrying too much of it. If adipose tissue, or fat, is the primary source of our weight then it's likely that weight loss is necessary for our health. Driven by both personal preference and health concerns, today's culture is increasingly focused on weight management and weight loss.

Every year there seems to be a new diet or weight loss trend. These trends can take the form of: new appetite suppressants, new energy and protein drinks to curb hunger, or new meal replacement plans. On top of replacement plans and dietary supplements available to purchase, there are plenty of popular diets making their way to the forefront.

Most recently, some such diets have become resistant to the word "diet" and are being presented as a "Way of Eating" (or WoE) in order to suggest that they are more a lifestyle than a diet. In addition to all of the weight loss supplements, diet aids, and eating plans, there has also been a rise in "weight-loss surgeries". With so many options and opinions available it is hard to navigate through what works, what is a gimmick, and ultimately, what will actually work for you, personally, long term. So, using my personal experience, my common sense, and my professional knowledge (gained through coursework I've taken as a personal trainer) I'm going to break down some of these options.

Weight Loss Surgery

The most seemingly radical of the options listed above is weight loss, or bariatric, surgery. Perhaps that is because all surgery comes with risk, however, we should be aware that sometimes the associated risk with continuing to carry excess weight outweighs the associated risk of surgery. Most people who undergo bariatric surgery have tried and failed, for years, to lose weight and have quite a bit of weight to lose. Bariatric surgery is, medically, considered the most successful intervention to aid in weight loss. This is attributable to that fact that these surgeries physically reduce the amount of food the stomach can hold. Bariatric surgeries have undeniable benefits since candidates have a legitimate medical need to lose weight. For some, these surgeries can improve every aspect of life; allowing better movement in daily activities, the ability to play with children, enhanced motivation for ministry, and even better sleep.

Unfortunately, as with any type of surgical procedure, bariatric surgery is expensive. The cost of these surgeries is further compounded by the fact that most insurance providers see bariatric surgery as elective unless the patient has a major medical issue. In fact, most people who apply for these surgeries are usually not approved by their insurance companies. Part of the reason behind low approval (although approval rates are rapidly increasing) for this surgery is that many would prefer to see a greater emphasis on prevention rather than treatment after an individual has gained excess weight.

Considering weight loss surgery, of any kind, is a big step, and while it has many life changing benefits, it is best to view it as a tool, and not a permanent solution by itself. Long term success with weight loss surgery, like anything else, is based on the ability to make healthy long term choices. Weight loss surgery is not the easy way out. It is physically and mentally challenging; especially because in both the short term and the long term, a new mindset is required to continue and maintain the weight loss. If you opt for weight loss surgery but continue to eat poorly and/or too much, you can, and most likely will, reverse the effects of the surgery. It is important to keep in mind that the long-term success is also strongly affected by the mind and spirit of each individual.

Prescription, Non-prescription, and Herbal Weight Loss Drugs

A seemingly less risky option for weight loss is the use of over the counter, or non-prescription weight loss drugs, and following right behind weight loss pills are herbal weight loss supplements. Please note, I say "seemingly less risky" for a reason. In my opinion, though there are studies to be found about the effects of prescription weight loss drugs, there is very little research about non-prescription weight loss drugs or herbal supplements that claim to aid in weight loss. Because there is little research about non-prescription drugs, we often don't know the effects until damage has been done to us or someone else.

Despite how good weight loss drugs and aids seem— prescription and non-prescription alike— there is no magic pill. Non-prescription weight loss drugs, like their prescribed counterparts, have to be tested by the Food and Drug Administration (FDA), but that doesn't automatically mean that they are safe. While it is not extremely common, non-prescription drugs and herbal supplements can cause health problems. In the 1990s Ephedra based drugs were extremely popular weight loss aids. Ephedra is a supplement derived from a bush and it was extremely effective, however, by late 2004 it became illegal to sell Ephedra based supplements due to the negative side effects associated with unregulated doses. Ephedra, once deemed safe and effective, was later found to be dangerous (something that does happen as studies and science progress). Today, derivatives of Ephedra can be found in some weight loss supplements since manufacturers have removed part of the herb that caused the most problematic side effects.

Whereas both prescription and non-prescription weight loss drugs have to be processed by the FDA, herbal supplements do not. As a result, even though the packages of many herbal supplements claim that the contents are "clinically proven", this may only be true in a very technical sense. In many cases, the manufacturers of these supplements are in charge of their own studies, meaning they may biased. Additionally, some of these supplements have multiple ingredients, often including caffeine, making it difficult to decipher which ingredient is actually aiding in weight loss.

At best, all these pills and supplements can do is aid in weight loss; they are not the fix. A reduced caloric intake and/or an increase in physical activity is still necessary for weight loss. A study done in 2016 on the effectiveness of prescription drugs showed a higher success rate of achieving a weight loss goal, but only when in combination with the proper lifestyle changes. Since herbal supplements, non-prescription aids, and prescription aids cannot work independently, and because the implementation of lifestyle change is still necessary, why bother with the risks or side effects of drugs?

Fad Diets and Trendy Ways of Eating

Arguably the least risky, and increasingly more popular, way of losing weight is changing the way we eat. This is done through different WoEs and often through meal replacements.

Meal replacement diets have been a favorite weight loss tool for many years. This is likely due to the fact that most of the plans available are easy, convenient to grab, and decisive—the need to meal plan or make food decisions is eliminated. These meal replacement plans often allow for one prescribed meal a day along with 2 meal replacements in the form of bars or shakes. Meal replacement diets are effective because they, by nature, limit caloric intake. Even though these diets often are good for jump starting weight loss, they are rarely ever successful long-term diets. This particular way of eating is probably the most restrictive because restaurants typically don't serve meal replacement bars and shakes. We live in a culture that dines out, and while restaurants may not have many available options for those who practice other ways of eating, there will be far fewer options for this type of plan. A meal replacement diet can be a good tool when combined with a long-term plan to resume eating real food, but alone it's not likely to yield positive long-term results. It is especially important to check in with your doctor before starting this kind of diet particularly because some of these dietary supplement shakes or bars, like herbal supplements, are not regulated by the FDA.

One of the fastest growing diet trends is the keto-genic diet (Keto). Over the past several years, the keto-genic diet has become increasingly popular, and while we tend to think of it as a trendy new diet fad, the fact is that this particular WoE has been around for centuries with different names and slight variations. In fact, low carb diets have long been utilized by medical professionals, along with traditional medicine, for treatment of some neurological conditions. The keto-genic diet is based upon eating moderate amounts of protein, high amounts of fat, and very low amounts of carbohydrates (usually less than 50 grams a day). This type of diet is also referred to as: the LCHF (low-carb, high-fat) diet or low carb diet. Staple foods of this keto diet include: fish, chicken, pork, beef, eggs, cheese, butter and heavy cream, avocado, and of course— bacon. Some people aim to have as much as 80 percent of their diet from fat with the remainder of their diet focusing on protein consumption. In contrast to fats and proteins, only minimal amounts of carbohydrates are eaten, and those that are usually come from condiments or vegetables.

The main premise behind this diet is to switch the body's primary energy source from carbohydrate to fat. The keto part comes into play because this type of diet forces the liver to break down stored fat to turn into energy, and release ketones which are the byproduct of the breakdown of fats. Part of the reason that some people are successful on a keto-genic diet is that the intake of foods high in fat and protein will often lead to feeling full and experiencing less cravings, resulting in a reduction of mindless snacking. During the first few weeks of any diet, it is fairly easy to lose weight while still eating quite a bit of food. With the keto diet part of this loss is because carbohydrates inherently hold water and a lack of carbohydrates causes the body to flush the extra water. While all of this is reasonably positive— even wonderful for those who love cheese and meat— there are some drawbacks.

The disadvantage of eating a keto-genic diet is the lack of fiber and other nutrients and/or vitamins. The inherent lack of fiber and other nutrients in a keto diet may make the use of supplements necessary if one isn't intentional about consuming a wide variety of foods rich in essential nutrients. Another disadvantage of a keto diet is that this way of eating, for some, can seem very restrictive. Consequently, keto is often not realistic as a long-term way of eating. Finally, in spite of the fact that keto-genic eating plans are not a new concept, there doesn't seem to be enough solid research on the long-term effects of the ketogenic diet in response to concerns about cholesterol, heart disease, or liver function.

Ultimately, although there may be many benefits to implementing this diet, because it is a stark departure from how most of us have spent our lives eating, it would behoove us to seek the opinion of a medical professional before engaging in a keto-genic diet. As I mentioned before, there is the potential for some adverse effects with this diet. Be sure to discuss the ketogenic diet with your doctor, and the effects of the diet on your organs and bodily functions; particularly your risk for high cholesterol or heart disease.

Historically, people who practiced a vegan lifestyle did so, for ethical reasons, as a lifestyle choice; more recently people have begun turning to a vegan diet to address health concerns. The vegan lifestyle was largely born as a form of protest against animal cruelty and the killing or exploitation of animals for any reason, including food and clothing.

Those who eat a vegan diet also reject the consumption of animal by-products such as eggs and dairy products. As with any diet, there are multiple variations of the vegan diet including, but not limited to: "raw vegan" which is raw produce alone, "the thrive diet" which is restricted to minimally processed whole foods, "the starch solution" that is focused on grains and potatoes and "the whole food vegan" that follows a plan of consuming any plant-based food that is un-processed.

Veganism is seemingly a simplistic diet and has a reputation for being one of the healthiest eating options out there, thus drawing more people to try it. There are, despite the whole food movement among vegans, those who rely heavily on processed vegan foods, meat replacements, vegan deserts, and lots of tofu to fill in their diets. Vegans who rely heavily on processed foods aren't much healthier than the average person; they also struggle with weight related issues. Most vegans, however, do tend to be thinner than those who eat a typical American diet of meat and processed foods.

Studies have shown the vegan diet to be more effective for weight loss than many other diets. This may be in part due to a lower caloric intake in response to the intake of high amounts of dietary fiber. High consumption of dietary fiber also keeps the blood's response to sugar, and by extension, diabetes in check. Healthy vegan diets also boast other health benefits such as: lowering the risk of developing hypertension or high cholesterol, minimizing the side effects and pain associated with arthritis, and (according to recent studies) a possible correlation with lowering the risk of Alzheimer's. It is absolutely true that the vegan diet has many wonderful benefits, however, there are a few things to be careful about while eating this way.

Vegans should be careful to avoid eating too many meat replacements because studies have shown that it is better to eat high quality meat than to consume too many processed soy replacements. Protein is a primary nutrient that our bodies need to build and maintain healthy skin and muscle tissue, among its other primary functions. There are plenty of plant-based proteins such as: beans, lentils, and whole grains; those following a vegan diet should be mindful to incorporate some of these proteins into every meal. Also, most vegans need a B-12 supplement, and possibly an iron supplement, as these are nutrients found predominately in animal proteins.

By way of disadvantages to this WoE, some would also argue that following a vegan diet is restrictive and time consuming in terms of meal prep. Finally, as with the keto diet, for many this would be a big leap from the way we traditionally eat and, although it seemingly lacks a significant change in organ function, as with the keto diet, it would still be best to consult with a medical professional before jumping into this way of eating.

The final diet plan, or way of eating I'd like to review in this section is steadily growing more popular with doctors— the Mediterranean diet. This WoE is primarily plant-based with an emphasis on consuming non-starchy fruit and vegetables, whole and sprouted grains, olives and olive oil, along with healthy fats. Moderate amounts of fish (rich in omega-3), dairy, poultry, and small amounts wine and sweets are also consumed on the Mediterranean diet.

This diet has been increasingly embraced by doctors since the 2013 study done by the University of Barcelona. The study consisted of more than 7,000 participants including a significant number of people who smoked, were overweight, or diabetic. In a span less than five years, the study determined that adherence to the Mediterranean diet contributed to a 30 percent reduction in cardiovascular risks even among those participants who we already high risk. This was especially ground breaking because fat has long been categorized as bad for heart health and the Mediterranean diet is rich in fat, however, it is important to note it is not rich in all fats. The Mediterranean diet stresses natural healthy fats as found in avocados, fish, nuts and olives, rather than fats typically found in processed food or red meats. Another thing to keep in mind is that even though this particular diet does not stress calorie restriction, the Mediterranean diet does practice healthy portion sizes. For instance, on the Mediterranean diet, instead of eating a whole avocado, you would typically eat a quarter or half of an avocado; likewise, instead of eating three or four handful of nuts you would only eat a small handful.

In addition to the cardiovascular benefits, another benefit of the Mediterranean diet is that it's rich in illness fighting antioxidants due to the its base of a large variety of fruits and vegetables. Because there is such a wide variety of foods to eat, people who choose this diet find it easy to stick with long-term. Though there are many benefits to this diet, there are some perceived negatives. First, it doesn't promise a double-digit loss in a week or two as is common with the other diets I've discussed. Second, the Mediterranean diet allows for a variety of food from every category, but doesn't give exact amounts to eat from each so therefore it isn't structured enough for some people. As a result of these perceived negatives, even though this diet is popular with doctors, it doesn't seem to be as popular with the general population.

While we've examined several weight loss trends and fad diets within this chapter, there are dozens other diet plans. For the sake of time and space allow me to point out that most diet plans work to some degree, but sustained success is largely based on long-term tactics. Over the years of losing weight I tried: Metabolife, Hydroxycut, Slim Fast, Special K products, Atkins or keto, veganism, and several other diets. The result was, yes, they all work. They work because they each find a different way to lower caloric intake—one of the key factors for weight loss—they are just different paths accomplish the same goal, and they each come with their own drawbacks. The most significant drawback is that they are not realistic plans for living the rest of our lives. I've had moderate success with many different diet plans. However, my journey of losing over 110 pounds, gaining over 60 pounds during pregnancy, losing that, and then maintaining my current weight for over 10 years, has taught me there really is no substitute for shifting the way that we think about food and the way that we live our lives. Each year my body grows leaner, stronger, and shows no sign of slowing down as I age because I've taken the time to strengthen my mind and spirit in order to support a holistic lifestyle change.

The key to choosing weight loss tactics is to find something that is focused on long-term results rather than a short-term loss. Many popular diets don't have long-term plans and instead encourage you to "jump in and stick with it". Likewise, many supplements and replacements don't have long-term instructions other than "reduce usage after reaching your goal and keep as part of your diet permanently". With respect to some of the diets we discussed, some people do stay on keto, vegan, or Mediterranean diets for their entire lives, but this is usually because an individual feels better physically and/or morally as a result of the diet. Very seldom do people trying these diets, merely for weight loss, stick to them for the remainder of their lives. The lack of sustainability is why many people yo-yo diet— constantly losing weight and then gaining that same weight (often with additional weight) back. This is also why so many have tried multiple supplements, replacements, and diets while searching for that one magical plan that will work.

Choosing the right plan for you can be overwhelming, and you may be able to avoid some of the trial and error with help from medical professionals. Seeking medical advice is always a great decision, especially if you already have some health concerns. You should not eliminate whole food groups from your diet without having good information on how doing so will affect your body. Additionally, you should be careful to choose the right plan for you without extensive experimentation, because hopping from one diet to another could potentially wreak havoc on your body. It's been my experience that some of the damage from reckless dieting can have long lasting consequences. Seeking medical advice, as well utilizing God-given wisdom will help guide you toward making the right decision.

Chapter Thirteen

Eat, Drink, and Be Merry

His divine power has given us everything we need for a godly life through our knowledge of him who called us by his own glory and goodness.

2 Peter 1:3(NIV)

Yes, God has truly given everything we need, every instruction that we need to lead a Godly life, and He made no exception when it came to eating. The Bible has plenty of information to offer about what we should eat— so much so that it is often debated between believers. Diet can be very personal to some and is usually influenced greatly by culture and by lessons learned from previous generations. While God's word does provide us with insight and information on how we should eat in order to honor Him with our bodies, Romans 14 reminds us multiple times that He never intended for His people to argue or to be divided over the subject.

Some people feel that their lifestyle best honors God by restricting their diets or by avoiding specific foods. Given that every body is different, and has different needs and/or health requirements, it may be wise for an individual to abstain from a specific food or food group, however, what we eat is not a salvation issue. Ephesians 2:8-9 says, "*For it is by grace you have been saved, through faith—and this is not from yourselves, it is the gift of God -⁹not by works, so that no one can boast*". We are not saved by what we do, or do not eat— we are saved by grace through faith.

The idea that we can somehow gain the favor of God by practicing dietary abstinence or that we can lose our positioning with God by consuming the wrong food, is usually passed down from previous generations. Alternatively, it is the result of either a misinterpretation or insufficient study of scripture. For example, there are some who believe that God intended us to be vegan. Often such people can point to scriptural evidence to support this claim; most often Genesis 1 is used in this fashion. In Genesis 1 God says that He has given "every green herb" for food thus implying (according to those who believe God wants us to be vegans) that our food should be plant based. While this might be a valid point when considered in isolation, God adds to this instruction in Genesis 9 when He speaks to Noah saying that every living, moving thing is given as food (just as the plant was). Misinterpretation and/or misunderstanding of God's word happens when we don't take the time either to understand context or to dive more deeply into a subject— this is why personal Bible study is crucial to the believer. When we don't study God's word for ourselves, we are subject to the teachings of those around us, and we really can't be sure about the source.

Another scripture that is often cited as evidence that the Bible instructed us to avoid certain food groups is Leviticus 11. Leviticus 11, found in the Old Testament, gives guidelines as to what food is clean or unclean. In the Old Testament, if God deemed a food clean, it was safe for consumption, and if God deemed food unclean it was to not to be consumed. Among the things deemed unclean in the Old Testament are: pork, shrimp, lobster, crab, and several types of bird. This part of scripture is what compels many people to give up pork, however, many of the same people who abstain from pork, based on this scripture only also miss (intentionally or unintentionally) the following chapter's ban on seafood. Yet another Old Testament scripture misused to justify a restricted dietary lifestyle is found in the book of Daniel. In chapter 1, Daniel and his friend decide not to eat the choice food offered to them from the king, instead they chose to eat only vegetables and drink only water. Verse 15 goes on to say that after eating this way for 10 days "*they looked healthier and better nourished than any of the young men who ate the royal food*" (Daniel 1:15 NIV). While this story from Daniel is an example of the positive outcomes of healthy eating, health is neither the focus of the story, nor the reason behind Daniel's choice. In both Leviticus and Daniel, the purpose of the restricted diet is to set God's people aside; it's more about purity and separating from the pagan culture of the time than health. In the Old Testament diet was one way the people of God honored Him.

In Old Testament scripture God's people used animals and food not only for nourishment, but also to honor God and to offer Him sacrifices for the remission of sin. The God given laws in the Old Testament, regarding food and animals, were used as a means of justification— that is to put God's people in right standing with Him. Today, we are all justified or given the opportunity to be in right standing with God, through Jesus, rather than through law. When Jesus came, He came as the perfect sacrifice; being the perfect sacrifice He fulfilled the Levitical law. So, what we choose to eat is not connected to our salvation.

[23] Before the coming of this faith, we were held in custody under the law, locked up until the faith that was to come would be revealed. [24] So the law was our guardian until Christ came that we might be justified by faith. [25] Now that this faith has come, we are no longer under a guardian.

Galatians 3:23-25(NIV)

***

For Christ is the end of the law [it leads to Him and its purpose is fulfilled in Him], for [granting] righteousness to everyone who believes [in Him as Savior].

Romans 10:4 (AMP)

Levitical law was established to set God's people apart, to bring awareness to sin, and to provide instruction for obtaining forgiveness for sin. Jesus has fulfilled all of the Levitical law— not just the laws about makeup and jewelry (Jeremiah 4:30), not just the laws about having to stay separated after giving birth (Leviticus 12:4-5), wearing clothing of blended fabrics or planting two different types of crops in the same field (Leviticus 19:19)— He came to fulfill all of Levitical law including the laws around food.

The mistake many of us make, around the understanding and application of the word of God, is that we often leave out the Holy Spirit. We ought not to read or live God's word legalistically or selectively, but through the lens and guidance of the Holy Spirit. As we learned earlier, the Holy Spirit will guide us in all things, especially in the understanding and application of God's word. As each of us learns and grows in God, our understanding changes. We should be ever evolving; our levels of faith and our understanding of God's word should be different 5 years from now than it is today. Romans 14 teaches that since we are continuously evolving (each of us at our own pace), we should be careful about passing judgement on other believers simply because we interpret God's word differently, especially since we have the common goal of bringing glory to God. Christ died and fulfilled Levitical law so that we don't have to get caught up in disagreements about insignificant things like what another believer will or will not eat.

The Weak and the Strong

14 Accept the one whose faith is weak, without quarreling over disputable matters.² One person's faith allows them to eat anything, but another, whose faith is weak, eats only vegetables.³ The one who eats everything must not treat with contempt the one who does not, and the one who does not eat everything must not judge the one who does, for God has accepted them.⁴ Who are you to judge someone else's servant? To their own master, servants stand or fall. And they will stand, for the Lord is able to make them stand.

⁵ One person considers one day more sacred than another; another considers every day alike. Each

of them should be fully convinced in their own mind.
⁶ Whoever regards one day as special does so to the
Lord. Whoever eats meat does so to the Lord, for they
give thanks to God; and whoever abstains does so to
the Lord and gives thanks to God.⁷ For none of us lives
for ourselves alone, and none of us dies for ourselves
alone.⁸ If we live, we live for the Lord; and if we die, we
die for the Lord. So, whether we live or die, we belong
to the Lord.⁹ For this very reason, Christ died and
returned to life so that he might be the Lord of both
the dead and the living.

Romans 14:1-9(NIV)

Romans 14:1-9 reminds us that what we do and
what we eat is ultimately done unto the Lord, God, so,
let us begin to have more healthy conversations
around the subject of diet/food. Romans 14:13 goes on
to admonish us to "*Therefore let us stop passing*
judgment on one another. Instead, make up your mind
not to put any stumbling block, or obstacle in the way
of a brother or sister." Bearing this in mind, let us sit
together and focus more on the hearts and the health
of those in our circles and a little less on what they
choose to eat. Let us stop trying to convince each

other to believe and behave the way we do and instead, seek more to understand each other. Let us not seek to immediately defend our positions but let us listen with open minds and with hearts that will allow the Holy Spirit to filter and lead. For after all is said and done, the goal is that we be healthy and that God be honored through our stewardship of our physical bodies.

Another area of concern in regards to what should or should not be consumed, and one that is often debated among believers, is alcohol. There are some scriptures that caution against the consumption of alcohol such as:

They must abstain from wine and other fermented drink and must not drink vinegar made from wine or other fermented drink. They must not drink grape juice or eat grapes or raisins

Numbers 6:3(NIV)

You ate no bread and drank no wine or other fermented drink. I did this so that you might know that I am the Lord your God.

Deuteronomy 29:6(NIV)

While these scriptures, and others like them, seem to speak against consuming alcohol, there are several other scriptures that seem to encourage the enjoyment of alcohol.

and I will bring my people Israel back from exile.

They will rebuild the ruined cities and live in them.

They will plant vineyards and drink their wine;

they will make gardens and eat their fruit.

Amos 9:14(NIV)

***

Go, eat your food with gladness, and drink your wine with a joyful heart, for God has already approved what you do.

Ecclesiastes 9:7 (NIV)

These verses of scripture seem contradictory and this seeming contradiction furthers the point that we must filter God's word through the Holy Spirit and dive deeper into subjects that do seem confusing. When diving deeper into God's word we discover that what the Bible seems to be most explicit about, with respect to alcohol, is not so much whether we consume it or not, but the effect it has on us when we begin to drink it too often or in large quantities. Becoming addicted to alcohol and/or drunkenness is sinful.

Woe to those who rise early in the morning

to run after their drinks,

who stay up late at night

till they are inflamed with wine.

Isaiah 5:11 (NIV)

***

[19] The acts of the flesh are obvious: sexual immorality, impurity and debauchery; [20] idolatry and witchcraft; hatred, discord, jealousy, fits of rage, selfish ambition, dissensions, factions [21] and envy; drunkenness, orgies, and the like. I warn you, as I did before, that those who live like this will not inherit the kingdom of God.

Galatians 5:19-21

***

⁹ Or do you not know that wrongdoers will not inherit the kingdom of God? Do not be deceived: Neither the sexually immoral nor idolaters nor adulterers nor men who have sex with men ¹⁰ nor thieves nor the greedy nor drunkards nor slanderers nor swindlers will inherit the kingdom of God.

1 Corinthians 6:9-10

The sin isn't in the drinking of alcohol, but in the overuse that results in drunkenness and addiction. However, those of us who do consume alcohol should be mindful not to cause another believer, who does not or cannot consume alcohol, to stumble. Too much alcohol will cause us to be ineffective in being able to win and lead new disciples for Christ by diminishing both our mental and physical health. Use and overuse of alcohol affects our mental alertness and our physical health. Under the influence of too much alcohol our minds become slow to react, our vision may blur, and our speech may become slurred, our judgement becomes compromised, we become unstable on our feet, and we may even pass out. Long term alcohol abuse can lead to unhealthy changes in weight, heart disease, or liver disease.

Beyond the detrimental effects that alcohol can have on our physical and mental health, remember overuse of alcohol can have negative effects on our spiritual being, and it may ultimately compromise our ability to reflect Christ. So, as believers we must be careful to remember that alcohol is not just a beverage— it is a drug, and we need to mindful how, when, and in what quantities we consume it. Overuse of alcohol will not allow us serve God nor will it demonstrate us honoring Him with our bodies.

Although what we choose to eat is insignificant, like alcohol God does provide us some parameters on the consumption of food. There are dozens of Bible inspired diets available to us. I call them "Bible inspired" because the Bible does not give an explicitly prescribed diet for God's people. However, the Bible tells us that gluttony (habitual over-eating) is sinful (1Corinthians 10:7, Philippians 3:19). Gluttony is not often addressed in churches, or even among peers, and that is simply because many of us are guilty of it. Furthermore, there are some of us that are really overtaken by gluttony. Gluttony is as much a sin as drunkenness, and the reality is that it is as difficult a habit to break as any other. Because food, unlike alcohol, is necessary for life, gluttony can be an especially hard area to gain control of without shifting to the opposite extreme. Food is also a major part of many cultures and so it is often encountered in various forms. Many television shows are focused on food, commercials advertise food consistently, and many of our gatherings are centered around food as well. We often connect through food and that is no surprise since God uses food in connection to our relationship with Him.

That each of them may eat and drink, and find satisfaction in all their toil—this is the gift of God.

Ecclesiastes 3:13(NIV)

Enjoying eating and drinking is a gift from God, and He wants us to enjoy these gifts. So, it would make sense that we would gather around these gifts, of food and drink, and share them with those we love. This may also be why feasts are given and described throughout the Old and New Testaments. Even in the book of Revelations (chapter 19) John describes his vision of the wedding supper in heaven that is promised to all who remain faithful to God. In the midst of these accounts of feasting, the Bible models for us moderation in all things, including alcohol and food. 1 Corinthians 6:12 says "'*I have the right to do anything,' you say—but not everything is beneficial. 'I have the right to do anything'—but I will not be mastered by anything.*"This scripture reminds us to be careful about being ruled by anything. For some, alcohol and food can be as much a god as money can. We must be careful to guard against allowing food or alcohol to become a god to us.

So yes, we should have a feast every once in a while, (not every day or even every week). It's alright to enjoy a piece of cake, or a glass of wine, or a beer— just be sure you have control over it and it does not have control over you. If you do feel that food or alcohol has some control over you, please contact your doctor for help immediately.

So whether you eat or drink or whatever you do, do it all for the glory of God.

1 Corinthians 10:31(NIV)

Chapter Fourteen

Dream, Discover Why, and Decide

When it comes to honoring God with our bodies, knowing and understanding is a great start, but next, we need to figure what changes we need to make in order to do it. When we aren't sure what changes we need to make, most often a look in the mirror, a glance through the medicine cabinet, and/or a visit to the doctor will pin point what changes are necessary. There are also those of us who already know what changes we need to make; in fact, we may have even attempted (and failed) to make them before. The main reason why so many of us don't achieve our goals is because when we set goals, we have unrealistic expectations about how long and how much effort it takes to achieve them.

The most common health goals that people set are: to quit smoking, to lose weight, and/or to gain muscle (increase lean body mass). The problem with these goals is that they are just dreams—often lacking a plan and a why. Every great dream should spawn a great goal, complete with a plan and a great "*why*". A great *why* is what will keep us on track and pressing forward to reach our goals, and the most successful *whys* are ones that are connected to God and to other people.

There is a "*God why*" for every believer. A *God why* is the result of the dream, desire, and purpose that God has embedded in each of us who are under the submission of the Holy Ghost. The fact that our health is important to God should make it important to us. The issue becomes that very few of us think that we can achieve the physical health, strength, and wellness goals needed to truly honor God. Therefore, we often settle for "okay" or "good enough". But, the truth is that not only can those of us who claim God as Lord of our lives achieve a personal level of health that is glorifying to Him, but we can also be happy doing it! Making changes that put us within God's will for our lives results in peace, joy and blessings. This is why we can be sure that we can succeed when changing our lives for better health— because it is God's will for us. When we care for our physical bodies we are displaying our thankfulness to God for them, for what they are able to do and for what they will be able to do. This is what it means to honor God with our sacred temples.

The fact is that our health is about more than us. Our bodies are the vehicles through which we move and produce; they are the tools that God uses to carry out His work here on Earth. Within each of us is a divinely placed ministry, a ministry that may bless 1 person, 10 people, or thousands of people. Ministry is part of who we are; even if we haven't figured out our ministry or purpose, we can be sure it is in us. It is that thing that draws us and shapes the desires of our hearts and minds. We should regularly seek God for direction, for purpose, and for vision of something BIG. For us, as believers, this ministry should become our dream, and since God is not the author of small dreams, this God given dream should be bigger than what we can accomplish on our own. This dream will require that we combine our giftings with God's resources. This dream should be our *God why.* This dream, this BIG dream, this *God why* should have longevity beyond our lifespan; it should have an impact that goes beyond our own personal interests.

In order for our ministry, our dream, our *why* to have longevity, it must be connected to people.

So we look not at the things which are seen, but at the things which are unseen; for the things which are visible are temporal [just brief and fleeting], but the things which are invisible are everlasting and imperishable.

2 Corinthians 4:18 Amplified Bible (AMP)

***

And now these three remain: faith, hope and love. But the greatest of these is love.

1 Corinthians 13:13 (NIV)

The Bible teaches us that only those things that are not seen (such as peace, joy, and love) last and that the greatest of these is love. Love happens in relationship with others; thus, building our *why* based on people ought to be part of our *God why.* If building on people isn't part of it, it's merely a dream or a wish, not a God given dream or a *God why.* We already know that for all believers, our ultimate purpose on Earth is to glorify God and to create new disciples as we reflect Him. How we do this, however, is completely unique to each of us. It is us up to us as individuals to spend some time with God seeking His purpose for us individually and learning our specific assignments. Our health is closely connected to our assignment. We cannot preach, sing worship songs, or praise dance with enthusiasm if we can't breathe. We cannot usher, do mission work, or care for the sick with joy if we cannot move freely.

Our being in good health also has implications beyond just the work of the church. We have assignment from God in every area of our lives. For example, we are assigned to be great parents, an assignment that undoubtedly includes: spending time with our children, playing, keeping up on school trips, and modeling behavior that is both Godly and healthy. But in spite of knowing our assignment we, as parents, often accept poor health for ourselves and sometimes we even allow our children to be in poor health, yet at the same time we never want them to feel what many of us do when we aren't comfortable in our own bodies. We don't want them to experience the despair of not being able to either keep up physically or do the activities they like to do. We wouldn't want them to feel badly about or in their bodies. Even though we can say many things to encourage our children to cultivate good health, we should pay much more attention to what they learn from watching us.

Poor health passes from generation to generation if it isn't checked. Those of us with children should take care of our health so that we can enjoy not only our children, but the generations of children after them. The same is true for aunts, uncles, older siblings, and cousins— all of these familial relationships help to mold the coming generations. The sad reality is that too many people die from preventable causes, thereby missing out on enjoying their time here on Earth. They lose time with their loved ones and sometimes even miss whole generations that they would have been able to welcome had their health been better. There was a time when great grandparents in their 80s and 90s were common to have around; it is now less common. Although the median age for great-grandparents goes down consistently (in part due to younger parents), some children have lost great-grandparents, and even grandparents, before forming memories. It is even more startling to hear reports indicating that as the years pass, younger generations may begin die before the older generations due to unhealthy lifestyles.

For young people, unhealthy lifestyles are modeled and enabled by the adults surrounding them. Whether we are parents, grandparents, aunts, uncles, cousins, ministry heads, community leaders, or church members, as people of God it is our assignment to move ourselves, and the coming generations, toward good health, to impart the importance of excellence in all areas of life, and to model honoring God with our bodies. No believer is exempt either from the influence of others or from influencing others. We all have an assignment to influence the next generation.

In addition to being on assignment within our sacred spaces we are also on assignment within our secular jobs. Therefore, we should be modeling good stewardship of our time and efficient work habits. It is easy to see how our physical health affects the quality of our work if we work a labor intensive, manual job such as: construction, loading or delivering packages, landscaping, security et cetera. But, we should not miss the ways in which our health can affect the timeliness and quality of work that is more mental in nature. For years, science has shown that our physical health affects our mental health and vice versa. Poor health often manifests in poor work, yielding stress; this stress contributes to bad health and starts the cycle again. It's a vicious cycle that many of us get caught in. Poor overall physical health, often due to lack of proper diet and regular exercise, contributes to how often we get sick with the common cold and other illnesses. Our bodies are less able to fight illness when they don't receive the proper vitamins and nutrients that come with a well-balanced diet (consuming burgers and fries, or pizza every day won't offer us any immune support). Low immunity leads to more illness, which results in either showing up at work but not producing timely, quality work, or taking time off of work, which yields the same results.

Studies have shown that people who eat a variety of whole foods daily are 25 percent more likely to have a higher job performance than those who have a diet of fast and processed foods. Additionally, those who exercise at least 30 minutes at least three times a week are 15 percent more likely to have a higher job performance than those who do not have a regular exercise schedule. So, let's follow this logic all the way through. Better health leads to better work; better work leads to promotion and more income; more income leads to more stability and thus, more opportunities for you (and your loved ones) to enjoy life and bless others. So, that raise that began with your better health has allowed you to pay off debt and release anxiety. That raise also enabled you to tithe more, which enabled the church to put much needed monies in their benevolence fund, a fund which was, in turn, used to pay the energy bill for a family with meager resources. As a result that family slept well that night without fear of waking up cold. That family will wake giving God thanks for the heart of His people who gave and for His provision for them. Next, that family will undoubtedly go on to bless someone else in their own way. Now, look at how your good health blessed someone else—someone you may not even know.

Whether we realize it or not, we are all connected to each other. Our respective influences go far beyond us— both for the good and for the bad. When we consider our health, and our *God why* that compels us to better health, we must be mindful of how our individual bodies affect the entire Body of Christ. We all have purpose in our homes, in our churches, in our workplaces, and in our communities. We must be fit to do God's work in every aspect of our lives. But sometimes, it can be hard to find the specific *why* that will push and motivate us. So, let us persistently seek God for greater vision, vision that causes us to do work that benefits us and that blesses those we are connected to (and beyond) so that ultimately God will get glory. We should persistently seek to find our people- based *God why* so that we can understand the role that our health plays in it— so that we can be prompted to change for reasons greater than vanity and greater than ourselves. Now that we understand the roles that God dreams and *God whys* play in our goal setting, let's apply that understanding as we turn our attention back to those common health goals that we identified in the beginning of this chapter.

Quitting smoking seems essential for good health, and it is. Smoking affects the entire body, especially our major organs, and its effects account for nearly one in five deaths. There are many reasons to quit smoking ranging from our own physical health to the health of those affected by our second-hand smoke and even to the health of our bank accounts. Physically, some of the most devastating effects of smoking show up in the form of various cancers. Additionally, smoking not only has devastating effects on the heart and lungs, but it also has detrimental effects on the autoimmune system, as well as bone and skin health. It is undeniable that smoking is extremely destructive to our temples and can prevent us from successfully working our assignments. Yet, for all of its negative effects, smoking is an extremely difficult habit to break because the nicotine is highly addictive. You need a coping plan and a quit date to go with your *why* if you want to be successful at quitting, and you may need some help from your doctor along with a support system.

Research has shown that those who quit smoking abruptly, with and without nicotine aids, have better success rates than those who quit gradually by reducing their consumption of cigarettes up until their quit date. So look at the calendar and set a quit date, and then share it with those who will be your support group. You must also decide how you plan to cope with withdrawal symptoms. Deep breathing, projects, gum, and snacks seem to be the most common coping mechanisms. To help manage the symptoms of withdrawal, there are a lot of smoking cessation aid available such as: patches, gum, and even some prescription drugs. Although the nicotine cravings may persist, the worst of withdrawal symptoms only last for a few days, up to two weeks. So, set that strong mind, sink some scripture into that strong spirit, and take control of your body. Honor God by taking steps toward stopping the destruction of your temple. If you need to quit smoking but are overwhelmed by the idea of getting started or of trying again, make an appointment with your doctor today.

Another common health goal is to lose weight. This goal may be self-explanatory if you are overweight, however, I encourage all of my clients who want to lose weight to be more specific because this goal also has implications on another common goal— to build muscle. Our body mass can be split into two categories – lean body mass (which includes our skeleton, organs and muscles)and fat. When it comes to weight loss we really don't want to part with any of our skeleton or organs, and muscle is essential for movement; this is all weight we want to keep, and even increase. So, if losing weight is our desire, what we really want to do is drop fat, and this is how we should frame and verbalize a weight loss goal. Losing weight can also include losing muscle mass and when we focus purely on dropping weight it is likely we will also lose some muscle. We should only seek to drop that which inhibits us from honoring God with our bodies and/or that which inhibits us from fully working our assignments—that, most likely, is fat and not muscle.

Muscle promotes movement and helps us complete everyday tasks, so we should always, at minimum, maintain our muscle mass. Dropping fat while maintaining muscle requires balance (which we will dive into more in the next chapter), and that balance needs to be reflected in our goals. In its most simplistic form losing weight boils down to achieving a daily caloric deficit over an extended period of time. In order to lose one pound, you must achieve a deficit of about 3,500 calories. Achieving that deficit is best done by a combination of restricting caloric intake (eating less) and exercising. This may sound simple, and the theory is simple, however, it is difficult to achieve a caloric deficit with the regularity necessary to achieve any significant weight loss.

Just as losing weight requires attention to diet and exercise, building muscle does as well. Although weight loss generally focuses more on diet, muscle increase often focuses more on exercise. Regular and consistent resistance training is necessary to build muscle and is often coupled with a higher caloric intake. While increasing caloric intake is common for individuals building muscle, the caloric needs are more individualized based on current weight, the amount of muscle desired, and the amount of strength training being done.

While we will go into more detail about healthy goal setting and how to achieve them more in future chapters, now is a good time to begin to dream and conceptualize yourself as you want to be. Recall your *God why* and ask yourself what sort of physical things you would like to be able to do but cannot do now. Begin to see yourself as strong, free, able-bodied, and confident. Then decide. Decide that you will be free in mind, spirit, and body. Decide you will be confident in every aspect of your life. Decide that you will be strong in mind, strong in spirit, and strong in body. Decide now! So, dream now, discover your *God why* now, and decide now who you are becoming.

Our desires should generally be shaped by personal ambition and divine inspiration. When, as we discussed in chapter 6, we are aligned properly with God, we can be confident that even our personal ambitions will not be outside of God's instruction for living. Being confident in that fact, we can be sure that He will provide the strength. As Matthew 7:7-8 tells us, if we ask we shall receive. Given that our physical health is key to both our well-being and our God-given assignment, we should not hesitate to seek God for help and intervention. But, at the same time, we must put our best effort into the area(s) we are seeking God's help with. Yes, with God all things are possible (Matthew 19:26), but we must be intentional about coupling that promise with James's reminder that "*Faith without works is dead*" (James 2:20). While God can give us strength and provide a way out of every temptation (1 Corinthians 10:13), He will only do so if we are doing our part. We should not expect God to help us desire vegetables when we just bought potato chips and ice cream, nor should we expect Him to help us desire water when we belly up to the bar. He will provide a means of escape from every temptation, but we have to have the right mindset to take it. For example, if we ask God to help us develop strong lungs for running, our part would be to quit smoking and/or go for a walk that actually challenges our breathing. Then, we need to put in sustained work by having a plan to increase our lung strength steadily. Similarly, we can ask God to help us develop a strong core or trunk muscles but we must be willing to do the exercises prescribed. We have to decide in our minds, despite our misgivings about ability, that we will start the work.

In order to accomplish creating a new health habit, we must have the persistence of a made-up mind. That made-up, persistent mind will encourage us when enthusiasm fades or results slow. That made-up and persistent mind will compel us to move outside of both our emotional and physical comfort zones. It will compel us to tackle a hill we aren't sure we can climb, to resist a craving that is overwhelming, to lift a weight that we are scared to try, to get on the floor to try an exercise when we aren't sure we can get back up; it may even compel us to hire a trainer who pushes so hard that we almost don't like them. It doesn't matter how many times we have tried and failed; we must try again. If the first ten minutes on the treadmill were hard, but if we aren't hurt, we get back on it anyway.

We must keep striving and keep persisting for those small gains — for those small wins— because they give God glory. The first ten pounds are lost by losing the first pound; the first 100-pound lift began first by lifting 10 pounds, and the resisting the first pack of cigarettes was overcome by resisting the first single cigarette. Ultimately, right decisions build strong minds, strong minds build strong spirits, and strong spirits build strong bodies. This process is circular and ever evolving. This circular process begins and ends with a dream, a belief, a decision, and persistence. We must rejoice in each win, no matter how small, and build upon it. Zechariah 4:10 cautions us to be careful not to despise small beginnings for the Lord shall rejoice to see the work begin.

When our desires and dreams line up with God's will, when belief spurs right decision and creates persistence, and when action meets God's power, victory is inevitable.

<u>Vision Check</u>: Take some time to write your God dream.

What are your top three assignments in life and how do they connect to your God dream? For instance, how does your God dream affect your ministry, your family, and your influence at work?

Translate your God dream, and its connection to your life, into your *why*. What about your dream compels you to want to change your life? What about your dream reveals the necessity of a physical change? That's your *why!*

Chapter Fifteen

Building Blocks

There are three foundational building blocks that shape our body composition. No matter our fitness level or health goal, each of these building blocks plays a part in achieving and maintaining good health; they are: nutrition, cardio (cardiorespiratory and cardiovascular) fitness, and muscular fitness.

Our nutrition is the primary, foundational block upon which everything else is built. What we eat affects how we feel, how we work, and what is reflected back at us from the mirror. Our nutrition refers to what we eat and how much we eat, and it is comprised of macronutrients and micronutrients. Micronutrients are specific dietary minerals and vitamins that, while essential for life, are consumed in small amounts. Intake and suggested levels of micronutrients are best assessed by a health care professional. Macronutrients are the three main nutrients necessary for sustaining life; they provide energy for us and are the source of calories. It is important to note as you move ahead that a calorie is not simply a calorie, the origin of your caloric intake affects your physiological response and your ability to meet your goals. Each macronutrient is metabolized and put to work differently in the body. The macronutrients are: carbohydrates, protein, and fat.

Carbohydrates

Carbohydrates (carbs) contain 4 calories in each gram and are the body's preferred source of energy because they are most efficiently converted into glycogen. Glycogen is primarily used as fuel for muscle movement (or exercise) and for the central nervous system. When carbohydrates are not used for energy, they are converted and stored as fat. Carbs are usually split into complex carbs and simple carbs; they are commonly referred to as good carbs or bad carbs respectively. Simple, or bad, carbohydrates have little to no nutritional value, and are most commonly found in processed foods and sugary deserts. Simple carbs cause the blood sugar to spike (or increase quickly) and then crash (or decrease quickly). The blood sugar crash is, in part, what causes cravings. In comparison, complex carbs have a slower and much gentler effect on the blood sugar. Because the increase and decease is slower with complex carbs, the energy produced is sustained longer and is more level.

Although some trendy diets deem all carbs bad, complex carbohydrates can be part of a healthy diet. Complex carbs in the form of fruit, vegetables, or whole grains are rich in fiber and antioxidants. Antioxidants support heart health as well as the immune system, while fiber is very filling. Eating complex carbohydrates that are low in calories and full of fiber is a wonderful way for us to fill up and fuel our bodies while supporting them. Although the standard recommendation is that children and most adults get 45 to 65 percent of their calories from carbs, the dietary needs of each individual should determine this percentage. Some of us may feel better eating a smaller percentage while some athletes may need to consume more. In my opinion there are very few times when non-athletes would ever need more than 50 percent of their diet to be from carbs.

Protein

While the necessity of carbohydrates is commonly debated, the necessity of protein rarely is. The importance of protein in our diets is undeniable and its functions are too numerous to list. Like carbohydrates, protein contains 4 calories per gram. Protein transports vitamins, nutrients, and fats to various parts of the body; therefore, it is key to brain development, as well as having healthy skin and hair. Protein is also responsible for creating enzymes and antibodies that speed our reaction time and fight illness. While protein is best known for aiding muscle development and function, it can also help keep hunger at bay. Protein, like fiber, is very filling and can help prevent overeating and cravings.

Protein exists in two varieties, complete and incomplete. Animal and soy proteins are complete proteins because they are the only proteins that contain all of the amino acids essential to maintain, build, and repair muscle and tissue throughout the body. Combining a variety of incomplete amino acids from a variety of plant-based foods is also an effective way to consume all of the essential amino acids. Given that the importance of protein is seldom debated it is somewhat surprising that the recommended dietary allowance for protein is just about 10 percent of our daily calories. However, many recent studies have shown that there are numerous benefits to increasing that level to about 30 percent, especially for people interested in gaining more muscle mass. I believe that more active people, people trying to lose weight, people interested in increasing muscle mass, and those concerned about the deterioration of muscle mass due to aging, would all benefit from eating a higher percentage of protein.

Fats

With more than twice the calories of carbohydrates or protein, fats are the densest of the macronutrients, containing 9 calories per gram. Fats aid in a variety of functions including (but not limited to) vitamin absorption and hormone production, as well as aiding in nerve function. Fats, like carbs, are usually broken into two types— good fats and bad fats. The good fats usually come from nuts, various kinds of fish, avocados, olives, and olive oil. While all fats are generally filling, good fats can boost the metabolism, and act as an aid to protein as well as aiding in vitamin absorption. Fats also perform many other functions, for example: soybean and cold-water fish contain essential fatty acids that can reduce inflammation and aid in eye and brain development. Bad fat usually comes from food that is high in saturated fat such as: red meat, full fat dairy, or certain tropical oils. These types of fats should be consumed in moderation. Trans-fat, often listed as "partially hydrogenated", is worse than saturated fat. Trans-fat is usually found in processed foods such as peanut butter, chips, and crackers. It would be best to avoid these foods most, if not all, of the time. Over-consumption of bad fats often leads to high cholesterol and various heart diseases. The American Heart Association (AHA) recommends consuming 25 to 35 percent of calories from fat. It's my opinion that, when consuming good fats, the AHA recommendation on fat consumption is spot on.

While the nutritional needs of individuals will vary in all cases, a thoughtfully selected balance of all three macronutrients can result in a healthy, sustainable dietary lifestyle. Proper nutrition, achieved by understanding what we should eat and how it affects our bodies, is essential for cultivating energy balance. Energy balance is part of the equation for any plan to change our body composition. Energy balance refers to the difference between calories consumed and calories burned. If we consumed more calories in a day than our bodies burn in a day, we would have a positive energy balance. Positive energy balance results in weight gain—which would be helpful for increasing lean body mass or muscle. It we consumed fewer calories in a day than our bodies burn in a day, we would have a negative energy balance. A negative energy balance results in weight loss. This information is vital to remember when considering exercise. I am a firm believer that everybody can benefit from both cardio exercise and strength training. While the frequency and intensity of exercise varies from person to person, every person can benefit from regular practice of both modalities.

One of the secondary building blocks of your body composition is cardio (cardiovascular and cardiorespiratory) fitness. Cardio exercises not just the muscles, which are the body's prime movers, but also the heart and lungs. The heart and lungs work hard to deliver nutrients and oxygen to working muscles consistently, so, keeping them strong is key for ease of movement. While cardio greatly improves heart health, it is most commonly used to manage weight; it does this very well because it is the most efficient way to burn calories. Because cardio is an efficient way to burn calories, it is also an efficient way to change body composition through weight loss. Cardio improves blood supply to the brain and muscles, improves mood, helps prevent heart disease, improves sleep quality, and increases stamina, among other things. It is recommended that most adults get 150 minutes of moderate cardio, or 75 minutes of vigorous cardio exercise spread over the course of a week. While individual schedules will generally decide the amount and frequency of cardio exercise works that best for the general population, those with specific fitness goals may need longer, more vigorous workouts. While all cardio increases the heart rate, moderate intensity cardio is generally marked by quickened breathing, a light sweat, and the ability to talk without pausing for breath during exercise. In comparison, vigorous exercise is marked by rapid breathing, sweat, and the need to pause for breath mid-sentence during exercise.

Cardio is fairly simple to figure out and it can be done just about anywhere. You can walk, jog, run, row, swim, or dance. Choose the activity that you enjoy most or do a combination of 3 over a period of 30 minutes. The most important thing is to get your heart rate and you rate of breathing elevated for at least thirty minutes. Keep in mind that cardiovascular and cardiorespiratory work is not just for people who need to lose weight; everyone should engage in activity that falls into this category. Increased heart health, lung capacity, and stamina allow us to set about each life assignment with vigor, bringing God glory.

Another secondary building block that shapes our body composition is muscular fitness. Muscular fitness is maintained and improved through strength training, and it is necessary for the muscular definition that so many of us seek after. Strength training is not just for body builders or athletes. As with cardio, everybody can benefit from regular strength training. Strength training both improves bone density and prevents the natural muscle loss that comes with aging. Even though strength training has most commonly been associated with muscle growth, it also can aid in weight management because it increases our resting metabolism, resulting in more calories being burned throughout the day. This type of training can also make activities of daily living much easier to navigate. Increases in muscle, bone density, and strength are a benefit to everyone no matter their assignment. Strength training is about more than muscle definition; it's about having the strength to live your dream fully.

It's recommended that healthy adults engage in strength training for each major muscle group of the body, twice a week on non-consecutive days. Each group (arms, legs, and trunk muscles) should be trained using multiple exercises, and the exercises should be performed for 8 to 10 repetitions. While many traditional gyms offer multiple machines for each major muscle group, there are plenty of exercises that don't require you to have access to a gym; and you can learn to master them anywhere using easy to find items. Free weights (dumbbells) and exercise bands have become popular for at home workouts and are easily found and purchased in many stores. I believe, however, that body weight exercises are the best way to begin any strength training regimen and they can also be done anywhere, but they have the added benefit of requiring no equipment. Some examples of body weight exercises are: squats, lunges, planks, pushups, and leg extensions. Within each of these exercise types, there are many variations to target different parts of the arms, legs, et cetera.

Nutrition, cardio work, and strength training are the three main building blocks that you will need to base your body re-composition plan on. Plans without building blocks are about as useful as structures without foundations.

Chapter Sixteen

Smart Goals with Strategic Plans

As believers, we know that nothing happens by accident, but everything is either God-ordained or God-allowed. Moving toward our God-ordained dreams and God-allowed goals requires us to take the time to gain knowledge. Once we have gained this knowledge, it will provide us with the base to develop smart goals and build strategic plans. Strategic plans, combined with the motivation we received upon realizing our *God why,* will propel us toward success.

As you move forward in attaining knowledge and building your strategic plan, please keep in mind that while I am providing you with the tools to build, it's always a good idea to review your plan with your primary health care provider before implementing it.

Weight Reduction

In theory, losing weight is simple, but actually losing weight can be hard, and unfortunately most people make it harder than it needs to be. In the previous chapter, we identified the lack of a strong motivating *why* as the most common reason that people fail to meet their goals. The second most common reason that people fail to meet their goals is a combination of having unrealistic expectations and/or over-aggressive plans. Unrealistic expectations are often the result of viewing too many "get slim quick" infomercials while over-aggressive plans are often the result of watching weight loss or makeover "reality" shows. Social media, especially as it becomes a marketplace, can also be a contributing factor to false perceptions about losing weight. While all of these mediums can be entertaining— even motivating, they most-times fail to provide enough information for the viewer to fully understand the process, much less to go out and replicate it.

A third, but equally significant, obstacle that prevents people from achieving and maintaining a weight loss goal is having the wrong mindset. I believe there is a very real difference between a weight loss mindset and a life changing mindset. A weight-loss mindset is one that has a pattern of thinking which says "I'll stick with this plan to lose the weight and then it's over", or "I'm finally going to fit my

favorite jeans again", or "I'll be happy when I weigh
___." This type of mindset is problematic for several
reasons. First, it is not the result of a strong *why*.
Second, it frames weight loss as burden. Third, even if
the goal is achieved, it is seldom maintained. A life
changing mindset is one which has a pattern of
thinking that says "Every week I am stronger and
more energized; I'm going to stick with this", or "I can't
wait to see how I feel when I reach my goal", or "I'm so
happy to be gaining control of body". A life-changing
mindset looks forward to getting more fit every year.
The life-changing mindset is focused on more than
what is culturally approved; it is more focused on
what is God approved and what makes you feel great.
It's focused on growing stronger in mind, spirit, and
body. It is focused on the whole picture and on
longevity, instead of the passing pleasure of seeing a
number on a scale. When it comes to a life-changing
mindset, the number on the scale is one measure of
success, not *the* measure of success. So, if you really
desire a lifelong change, if you really desire to lose
weight and never gain it back, then you need to make
sure you have the right mindset. The right mindset
should be reflected in the process that you use to

achieve your goal. Keep your goal realistic and be strategic in your planning.

When setting your ultimate weight loss goal, it is important to be aware of what is influencing the determination of that particular number. Are you being influenced by a friend or something that you read? Or, perhaps you chose a weight you remember feeling good at. Maybe you're following the recommendation of a doctor. While these things may be good factors to consider when setting goals, you must guard against letting these influences overshadow your *why*. Instead, keep that God dream in the forefront of your mind. Your *God why*, shaped from your God-given BIG dream, should always supersede everything. Your *God why* encompasses all that God has purposed you for; if you do your part, He will do His and help you succeed. Your doctor may recommend losing 30 pounds, but you aren't losing them for him. Losing weight is about your health, your body, your life, your longevity, and your assignment. You drop 30 pounds for you and for how it's going to change not only your life, but also the lives of those connected to your *God why*.

Don't be fooled into thinking that a drastic change won't affect those close to you. Any significant weight loss will have both positive and negative effects on those around you and on your relationship with them. It will also change your perspective and cause you to cherish all of the positive effects in relationships. Keeping that God dream in the front of your mind will allow you to: dismiss the negative, stay focused, and be joyful. That God dream should also be the key factor that compels you to do what is in the best interest of your health and helps you to determine how much weight to lose. Once you have decided the amount of weight you would like to get rid of you're ready to start planning.

Setting a Weight Loss Goal

All things being equal, any person can ditch weight with simple math, diligence, and discipline. I, along with many professional health care providers, recommend aiming to lose one to two pounds a week, however, it is important to note that people with larger amounts of weight to lose may shed the initial pounds more quickly. In order to set a smart weight loss goal, you must first decide how much weight you want or need to lose.

If your weight loss goal seems daunting it's a great idea to set a smaller sub-goal to get started. Say you weigh 264 pounds and you want to lose 100 pounds; this may seem like a lot and be overwhelming. In a case like this, it may be good to break your ultimate goal into increments. What has worked with many of my clients (with larger amounts of weight to shed) is setting a weight loss goal that is more quickly attained than their ultimate goal. So, if we were developing a plan for you, instead of focusing on the ultimate goal of losing 100 pounds, we would pick various incremental goals from the starting weight of 264. The first goal may be for you to get down to 232 pounds, at which point you would just maintain for specified amount of time. The maintenance period allows for a more relaxed eating plan and provides your mind and body with a break. The next goal would be for you to weigh in under 200 pounds. When that goal is achieved, we would keep going to capitalize on positive energy and motivation until hitting 178 pounds. Then, again, we would pause for maintenance. In this manner we would continue on until reaching the initial goal. Not only is an incremental approach to weight loss often successful, it is not uncommon for clients to surpass their initial goal using this method. The point is that if the idea of dropping all the weight you want or need to lose is overwhelming, you should pick a smaller sub-goal; you can always set another.

Creating a Caloric Deficit

Having decided how much weight to lose and bearing in mind that a 1 to 2-pound loss per week is the recommended rate for safe and sustainable weight loss, you can use simple math to figure out approximately how long it will take to achieve your goal. For example, if your goal is to lose 50 pounds, you can estimate that it will take 25 weeks (or about 6 months) to achieve that goal. As I mentioned earlier, those with more weight to lose sometimes shed their initial pounds more rapidly. Since 50 pounds is a significant amount of weight, you may wind up closer to 22 weeks depending on your body fat percentage. If you aren't in a particular rush to lose the weight and prefer to go a bit slower in exchange for more dietary flexibility, it could take double that time. How much you lose over the course of a week or a month boils down to the energy balance that you create. Remember, if you want to drop weight you must create a negative energy balance, or a caloric deficit. Creating a negative energy balance, or caloric deficit, is achieved by burning more calories than you have consumed. In order to reach your weekly and monthly weight loss goals, you must strive to achieve a caloric deficit through the course of a day and/or a month. Bearing in mind that in order to lose 1 pound you must achieve a caloric deficit of 3,500 calories, here is how you can figure out your desired daily caloric deficit:

Creating your Desired Daily Caloric Deficit

Step one: (lbs x 3,500) / wks = WCD

Step two: WCD/7= DCD

OR

Step one: (number of pounds to drop x 3,500) divided by your set number of weeks = weekly caloric deficit needed

<u>Step two</u>: weekly caloric deficit/7= daily caloric deficit needed

Let's calculate the DCD (daily caloric deficit) necessary to lose 30 pounds in 20 weeks.

<u>Step one:</u> (30x3,500)/20= 5,250

First multiply 30 by 3500

Next divide that by 20 to figure out the WCD (weekly caloric deficit)

<u>Step two:</u> 5,250/7=750

Divide 5,250(WCD) by 7 to figure out the DCD

750 is the desired daily caloric deficit

Women should not consume less than 1,200 calories a day and men should not consume less than 1,500 calories a day. Women should aim to consume 1,500 calories a day for weight reduction (depending on activity level) and men should aim to consume 1,800 (also depending on activity level). Both, personally and professionally, I've found it's best to create daily caloric deficit by splitting it between calories consumed and calories burned. So, if you need a caloric deficit of 1000 calories a day, then 500-700 of those calories should come from reducing the calories you consume, while staying above the minimum caloric suggestions for you. The remaining 300-500 calories should come from increasing your daily activities and, more specifically, from your workouts.

Eating with a Plan

Aiming for a realistic caloric deficit is critical to having an eating plan that you can stick to. One of the biggest usurpers of calories is sweet, fat-filled, over processed food such as: candy bars, cookies, potato chips, and the like. When helping my clients find ways to cut calories, these kinds of foods are the first that I advise them to avoid. You want to plan to eat in a way that promotes weight reduction and allows sustained adherence. Over processed foods trigger cravings and, once consumed, do not leave you feeling full for long. If you're constantly feeling hungry, it isn't likely that you'll be able to adhere to your dietary plan for any real length of time because constant hunger will eventually drive you to break your plan. To combat feelings of hunger, you need nutrient dense, minimally processed foods that will keep you feeling well fed and energized.

In addition to eating filling foods, it's also a great idea to consume a wide variety of foods that fall within your dietary plan. I don't recommend cutting out any one particular macronutrient, but rather eating a good balance of each. Within each macronutrient group there are great options and there are less than great options; usually the less than great options are less great because of the way that they are prepared. Take chicken for instance. Chicken is a great source of protein whether it's grilled or fried, but grilled chicken will likely have less calories and fat, especially if it is a chicken breast as opposed to chicken wings. Likewise, all rice can be a great source of energy, but brown rice is a better choice because it won't spike your blood sugar as much as white rice will. Another good example to consider is salad greens. Salad greens are low in calories, and can be filling, but a spring mix of greens is a better choice than iceberg lettuce because it has more fiber and is nutrient dense. Finally, we all need fats, but, as we learned earlier, not all fats are created equally. Ultimately, you want to achieve your caloric intake goal by eating a variety of good, nutrient dense foods in proper portions. If you are unsure about how many calories you are eating, consider using an app to track your caloric intake on your phone, or track using a notebook along with a food scale until you really have a solid idea of how you are consuming.

Unlike proponents of the many get thin quick programs or trendy diet plans that exist, I do not believe one size fits all in any area of life. While that one size may be worn by all, not everyone wears it well. The same is true for nutrition. Anyone can lose weight on a calorie reducing plan, but not everyone will feel good on that plan. As I stated before, in the interest of sustainability, I usually suggest eating all macronutrients, however, some people function better with higher protein intake while others function better with higher complex carb and fiber intake. So, once you have determined your daily caloric goal, go back and work with the suggested macronutrient percentages to figure out what will work best for your body. It may take several weeks of tweaking to find what works for you. If you are overwhelmed doing this, your health care professional can likely recommend a nutritionist who can get you started, or you can turn to a qualified health or fitness professional for some advice.

Aside from eating, another area in which many people spend unnecessary calories is what they choose to drink. For my clients, I usually recommend limiting drinks to mostly water and some coffee or tea with minimal, or no, added cream or sugar. Drinking fewer calories will usually result in a higher consumption of water, which has numerous benefits and is a great goal for everyone. I find that in most instances there really isn't any reason to drink any calories (with the exception of a protein shake). While juicing has become pretty popular, you would be better served by actually eating the fruit (and vegetables) that you're juicing. In almost every circumstance, you juice more fruit than you would actually eat. Furthermore, when you juice, you tend to leave behind the part of the fruit that holds the most fiber. Missing out on the fiber content of fruit, in combination with elevated consumption, can lead to a spike in blood sugar similar to one that a simple carbohydrate would cause. In contrast, making smoothies, when done right can be beneficial. While juicing often discards the pulp and skin of fruits and vegetables, most smoothies actually incorporate them, thus, retaining more nutrients and fiber. Smoothies with fruit, greens, and a source of protein can be great meal replacements. When you put thought into building a good smoothie it won't be overloaded with calories, it will leave you satisfied for hours and it will even taste good. While adjustments can be made based upon preferences, I normally suggest starting with 1 cup of fruit (such as strawberries or sliced bananas), 1 generous handful of greens (spinach blends very well) and 1 scoop of protein powder. Such smoothies should be considered a replacement for something, rather than in addition to your normal meals or snacks if your goal is to minimize calories.

Plan to Keep It Real

Part of having realistic expectations is also knowing that you likely won't be perfect while following your dietary plan. It is likely that at some point you will either eat or drink more than you intended or consume something that isn't on your plan at all. When that does happen let it go and be careful to not compound it by accepting defeat. For instance, if you go to the movie theater and eat half a tub of buttery popcorn, don't then go out for dinner, have a few drinks, and eat off your plan just because you feel like you messed up already. One meal may undo a day as far as your caloric deficit goes, but that's about it. One bad meal won't instantly make you fat just like one good meal won't instantly make you skinny. One bad meal isn't an excuse to take time off from your plan. Two, three, or six meals will start to show up in your body composition and the scale though— it's the cumulative effect of what we eat that causes change. While you should not get stuck in your missteps, don't let yourself be okay with the 80/20 or the 90/10 rule— the rule that says that you only have to operate at 80 or 90 percent. These types of rules, that say you only need to be on your plan 80 percent of the time, don't promote long term success and often lead to back sliding. So, don't settle there. Consistently giving 100 percent of your effort to sticking to your plan is vital to your success. 80 percent effort can quickly turn into 50 percent. One cheat meal turns into a cheat day, and then after a few days, it's: "I'll start again Monday". Lack of consistency will result in slow or negligible results. Poor results will lead to poor morale, and ultimately, you will not follow through to achieve your goal. Planning to not follow your plan is not going to lead to success; you must plan to follow your plan 100 percent of the time.

Plan to Workout

A strategic weight loss plan is part nutrition and part exercise. While cardio, or aerobic exercise, has long been touted as the go to method for weight-loss, I believe a combination of both aerobic exercise and strength training provide the best long-lasting results. If you are new to exercising, you may have to build up to the recommend exercise guidelines in 5-minute intervals. That's okay; just start building! If you are able, and if you have a goal of weight reduction, I would suggest 30 minutes of moderate exercise 5 days a week, building to vigorous aerobic exercise 2 or 3 of those days. The modality, or type, of aerobic exercise that you do is up to you and is dependent on any injuries or contraindications (reasons to refrain from a particular exercise) that you may have. I usually recommend changing your modality of exercise every few weeks. Keeping the cardio fresh can be done either by switching modalities or adding intervals to your current exercise.

In addition to 5 days of aerobic exercise, you should also plan for 2 days of strength, or resistance, training. This can be done on 2 separate days or stacked onto 2 of your cardio days. Strength training should be done on non-consecutive days. If you're just beginning, you will likely only do two strength training sessions a week, and therefore, each session should be full body. A good full body session will include exercises for all of the major muscle groups— the lower body, the trunk, and the arms. Within each of these groups, there are many muscles, and it is important to create balance between opposing (or opposite) muscles. For example, if you work the quadriceps (the front of the thigh), you should work the hamstrings (the back of the thigh); if you work the biceps (the front of the upper arm), you should work the triceps (the back of the upper arm), and you should not only work the abdominal muscles, but the back as well. Try starting with 2 exercises for each muscle and work up to doing 3 sets of 10 repetitions of each exercise. For example, if you are training the muscles in your arms, you would do 3 sets of 10 bicep curls followed by 3 sets of tricep kickbacks, or 30 of each exercise with a break between each set of exercise. As you try to familiarize yourself with the kinds of strength training exercises available to you, it would be a good idea to do a little research, or better yet, purchase one or two private sessions with a trainer. As you get stronger, you can begin to rotate or add exercises for more variety. As with the aerobic exercise, you may need to start with a smaller goal such as 5 repetitions and build up.

Using all of this information to make an exercise plan may seem daunting, but as you are beginning, try to keep it simple. Be mindful, however, that if you are vigorously training, you will need a more detailed schedule that includes rest days. For beginners, your schedule for the week could be as simple as:

- ➢ <u>Monday</u>: 30 Minutes of Cardio (outdoor walk or treadmill)
- ➢ <u>Tuesday</u>: Strength – Full Body (3 muscle groups – 2 or 4 exercises each)
- ➢ <u>Wednesday</u>: 30 Minutes of cardio (outdoor walk or treadmill)
- ➢ <u>Thursday</u>: 30 minutes of cardio (hike, or stair climber, or hills)
- ➢ <u>Friday</u>: Strength – Full Body (3 muscle groups of 2 or 4 exercises each)
- ➢ <u>Saturday</u>: 30 Minutes of cardio (outdoor walk or treadmill)
- ➢ <u>Sunday</u>: 30 minutes of cardio (rowing)

Alternatively, you can stack Tuesday's and Friday's strength workouts onto two other, nonconsecutive cardio workouts to create a couple rest days.

When you're developing your weight loss plan, it is better to start simple. Simple is still very effective. Make sure to write your workout plan down and hang it where you see it multiple times a day. The same can be done with your eating plan. It can be helpful to write down your caloric goals and even make yourself a list of easy meals for those moments when you're feeling rushed or indecisive. Keep it simple, keep it consistent, and the results will come.

Increasing Muscle, or Lean Body Mass

While strength training can produce positive changes in body composition and increase the number of calories burned through a day, science has yet to prove it effective for weight loss. Common reasons for strength or resistance training are: to avoid muscle loss as years pass, to increase muscle mass for physique goals, to build muscular endurance, to build enough strength to accomplish a goal (such as a set of pull ups), or to compete in power lifting sports. Some even strength train for general health purposes with little to no desire for physical change. While each of these reasons requires more specific programming than what is intended in this book, I would like to broadly address the topic. I must specifically address the concepts and misconceptions that apply to all strength-oriented goals.

With all strength training goals you should consider the law of specificity. That is to say: what you train is what will grow. If you do bicep curls, the biceps will grow; bicep curls will not help you develop defined shoulders or a strong back. Using that logic, let's say you want to do pull ups. If your goal is to do a set of pull ups, you would train the muscles used in pull ups. The primary movers for under hand pull ups (chin ups) are the biceps and latissimus dorsi (triangular muscle groups on either side of the spine under the shoulder blades). These primary movers are assisted by muscles in the forearm and the muscle in the abdomen. Thus, to achieve a chin up you would specifically train the biceps and latissimus dorsi as well as the abdominal muscles. Doing lat pulls or bent over rows will help build the latissimus dorsi and aid you in reaching your goal. The law of specificity applies to any goal. What you specifically work, will work. This rule is also applicable to the various training protocols for your specific strength training goal; for example, training for power lifting is vastly different than strength training for overall wellness.

Another concept to keep in mind when it comes to any exercise is regularity. If you want to experience muscle gains you must work the muscles regularly and consistently. However, you should never do the same weight lifting program on 2 consecutive days. The muscles that have been worked should always have "rest days" so that they can recover before being worked a second or third time. If you're new to strength training, you should start with two or three full body sessions a week. Intermediate lifters, with basic skill, should begin to spilt muscle groups by days and train 3 to 4 days a week, while advanced lifters may work anywhere from four to seven days a week depending on their program.

As you move from being a beginner to being an intermediate lifter, progression and overload become important. This might be a great area in which to learn from a personal trainer. Asking a trainer at your gym, purchasing a few private sessions, or making an appointment with a virtual trainer could give you valuable insight into proper progressions and overload. Systematically increasing repetitions and weight (progression) and applying overload to fatigue to the muscles is crucial to continuing to see gains in strength, endurance, power, and mass. These concepts become especially important as you approach your size and strength potential as is dictated by your genetics. As you approach your potential, you will begin to notice diminishing returns—that is, your results will slowly decline within your program. Do not let diminishing returns lull you into thinking that you have no more room for growth or, worse yet, cause you to quit. Muscle has an amazing ability to deteriorate quickly. People who regularly train can expect to lose strength at half of the rate they gained it. This means, if it took you 12 weeks to acquire your gains, you will lose half of them in 12 weeks, and all of them in 24 weeks without exercise. This muscle loss is especially important for anyone over the age of 30 to be aware of. While most adults reach their muscular peak between the ages of 30 and 40, inactive adults can lose as much as 5 percent of their muscle mass every 10 years. Medically, this is referred to as sarcopenia. The rate of muscle loss steadily increases as the years go by— accelerating more after 50 and having debilitating results between the ages of 65 and 80.

If you lift often and build muscle, chances are you want to see it. One common misconception about muscle visibility is that if you lift heavy and often enough, you will develop a perfectly chiseled body. Yes, lifting heavy and lifting regularly will grow muscles however, they will not be visible if you aren't conscious of your body fat percentage. Typically, men need a body fat percentage under 10, and women under 20, to see that coveted six-pack. Although doing planks and leg lowers will strengthen the abdominal muscles, if you really want those abs to show, you may need to drop some body fat. While building muscle is subject to the law of specificity, weight management is not. You cannot target weight reduction to specific spots. Doing more lunges can build the quads, and while it may contribute to weight loss, it will not specifically burn the fat on your thigh any more than crunches will specifically burn abdominal fat. If you want to see those muscles be more visible, target your body fat percentage. If you're gaining muscle, but not losing fat, you are creating more body mass; although the muscle mass is lean and great, it is still more mass overall.

On the subject of mass, I'd like to dedicate this paragraph to everyone who believes that a woman lifting anything heavier than five pounds will result in her becoming bulky. The reality is, unless women are specifically aiming for a body builder physique, they likely will never have one. Female body- builders do an incredible amount of work, exercise amazing amounts of self-discipline, and can spend years creating their physiques. While women can increase muscle mass and muscular strength, and/or endurance, most women are physiologically incapable of easily achieving a bulky, or body builder, physique due to their hormonal makeup. Because it is difficult to achieve that physique, it is extremely unlikely that a woman would achieve that look by accident. Men have much higher amounts of testosterone, are generally larger, and have more muscle tissue. Plenty of men have purposely pursued a body builder physique and have found it either elusive or hard to achieve. How much harder, then, would it be for women? Women, as well as men, need to strength train regularly.

Creating the right energy balance to gain muscle is a bit more involved than creating the energy balance necessary for weight loss. If you are lifting in order to increase muscle, or lean body mass, then it is likely you will need a caloric surplus on the days that you lift. However, as in the case of weight reduction, what you eat is important. Six packs are built in the kitchen. While it is important to eat a bit from each macronutrient group, the focus for lifters needs to shift more toward protein. Since protein is critical to building and repairing muscle, it is important to make sure you are getting enough to fuel your muscle gains. The most commonly used ratio for protein consumption recommendations is 0.8 grams of protein per pound of body weight. So, if you're lifting for gains, 0.8 is the best ratio to start with *if* you have healthy kidneys and no other contraindications. A consultation with a nutritionist is the best way to go for figuring out your specific dietary needs. That being said, a common way to figure out your caloric needs for lifting is to multiply your weight by a given percentage; however, this will not be good for you unless you are already at your ideal weight *and* your caloric intake actually matches your workload. A

266

safer way would be to add about 300 calories a day on your lifting days. Make sure you are eating quality food from all the macronutrients and remember to be consistent.

Make Sure to Drink and Sleep

As you begin to move forward in developing your dietary and exercise plans, don't underestimate the value of water and sleep to your health. There are numerous benefits to drinking water, so make sure to get plenty of it. Water is essential to kidney function and to the breakdown of vitamins, and minerals; it supports joint health, and helps flush waste out of the body. Drinking plenty of water can also aid in managing caloric intake— turning to food is often the mistake made when what your body really needs is water. Staying hydrated also promotes healthy skin.

Sleep, like water, is essential for optimal health. Although the average adult needs between 7 and 9 hours of sleep, most adults don't actually get enough sleep. You know you aren't getting enough sleep if you are experiencing: mood swings, foggy memory, an inability to effectively multitask, or fatigue while driving, reading, or watching television. Exhaustion will also cause an increase in caloric consumption, and these calories are often from poor quality foods. If you commonly binge late in the evening, or at night, there's a good chance that you are really just tired. Getting an adequate amount of sleep will lead to better brain and muscle function, improved disposition, and lower levels of stress.

Chapter Seventeen

Detox and Move

The word detox as a verb is defined as: to abstain from or rid the body of toxic or unhealthy substances. I believe some sort of detox is beneficial to our minds, spirits, and bodies. In our minds we can find ourselves with toxic thinking patters, in our spirits we can locate substances that aren't of God, and in our bodies, we can see the evidence of substances that aren't beneficial to us. Although we often think of detoxes as deprivation for our physical bodies, everyone can benefit from a detox in their minds and spirits as well as in their bodies. If we truly desire good health in any one area of our lives, it's essential that we work toward good health in all of these areas.

It's common to hear the phrase "Mind, Body, and Spirit", but as believers we must begin to reorganize this to "Mind, Spirit and Body". What we put into our brains trains how we think, what we think influences what we believe, and our bodies often reflect how we think and what we believe. Similarly, how we feel, both physically and emotionally, has an impact on how we think and what we believe. Consequently, we must take the time to ensure the strength of these aspects of our beings. When our minds, spirits, and bodies are all working harmoniously, we will find ourselves living and enjoying life the way God intended for us to do.

You are Strong and Sound in Mind

Being strong in mind is about understanding who you are and how you think. It requires being aware of what compels you to action and/or inaction. Most of life's battles are waged in our minds. Recognizing flawed thinking patterns—where they stem from, and how they affect you— will allow you to begin strengthening your mind and controlling your mindset. Letting go of flawed thinking, fear, and un-forgiveness is more than just saying you'll do so; it also requires some action. If you struggle with depression, or if you've realized that you have flawed thinking patterns, I sincerely hope that you have reached out for help. If you haven't, put this book down and do that right now. It is impossible to live your life as God intended if you're struggling with depression, fear, or un-forgiveness. Detoxing the mind is about ditching flawed thinking patterns and freeing yourself from fear and un-forgiveness.

If you need to detox from, or rid yourself of, fear you must first acknowledge that fear is present. Remember, it manifests in lack of movement or in regression to poor habits. Look for the pattern of fear and trace it to its root. In what circumstance did you first find yourself afraid; why were you afraid? At the root you will find the enemy and/or someone else's flawed thinking. Next, acknowledge who God is and what His word says about you. He has not given you this spirit of fear; He has given you a sound mind. Your victory over fear lies in prayer, and don't simply go it alone; connect with a stronger believer. Your friends may already know your situation and if they could help you overcome it, they would have already done so. Try connecting with a pastor, an elder, a deacon, or a deaconess. Be open with that person and enable them to pour into you freely. Don't let shame stop you from obtaining victory and vision. Inject faith into fear and walk in that faith!

If you need to detox from, or free yourself from, un-forgiveness, just remember that there is a cost to holding on to un-forgiveness. It costs you your own forgiveness from God, and it also taxes you physically. The debt paid by forgiveness doesn't belong to you, but it belongs God. Jesus not only died so that you can be forgiven, but also so that others can be forgiven. The same blood that works for you works for your enemies too. Pray for them. Remember, forgiveness is a choice. Stop rehashing offenses and begin to speak well of those who have hurt you.

Pray about the hurts that cause fear, depression, and un-forgiveness and God will certainly capture your heart. When God has your heart, you will have the strength to take captive every thought and bring it into submission under God. Submitting depression, anxiety, fear, and un-forgiveness to God, time and time again, will pave the road of a strong, sound mind.

We demolish arguments and every pretension that sets itself up against the knowledge of God, and we take captive every thought to make it obedient to Christ.

2 Corinthians 10:5 (NIV)

<u>*You are Strong in Spirit*</u>

Being strong is spirit is about having a solid relationship with God. That relationship, like any other, is built upon trust, and trust comes with knowing someone. Unfortunately, many believers either don't truly know God, or they have a distorted view of who God is. Your view of who God is ultimately shapes who you are. Self-image is created from the cumulative effect of what you see, learn, and practice daily. Habits and thought patterns that we practice daily are built upon what we believe. You must teach yourself to believe that God divinely designed and destined you. He planted you as seed. You have the capability to produce good fruit. When Jesus warned of false prophets in the Book of Matthew, He also taught that good trees cannot bear bad fruit, and bad trees cannot bear good fruit. Thus, as a good tree you will either bear good fruit or no fruit. You do not want to become a barren tree. Biblically speaking, barren trees are usually destroyed. When you are "growing" among weeds and bad trees, it is vitally important that you guard against becoming permissive or complacent with popular culture (and therefore barren). The only way to produce good fruit is to grow. The only way to grow is to connect to God and learn who He is.

As you align and connect with God through prayer, and as you learn, through study, more about who He is and who He created you to be, you will naturally begin to detox your spirit. You will begin to pay closer attention to what you are feeding your spirit. Your spirit will begin to recognize bad doctrine and manipulation of the scripture. The sad truth is that there are too many believers ingesting bad spiritual food because their spirits are not as strong as they should be. The more personal time that you spend with God and in His word, the stronger your spirit will be. It is the same principle as feeding your body, eating fast or easy food can make you sick because you don't know how it has been handled and prepared. Likewise, failing to prepare the majority of your spiritual sustenance may sometimes lead to illness.

Being strong in spirit is foundational for living life God's way. The strength of your spirit is too important to depend on other people to nourish it. Regularly nurture your spirit through study and prayer. Seeking God, first for yourself, strengthens your spirit. For we, as believers, greatness is accomplished not by our own might, but by the Spirit of God.

> *6 So he said to me, "This is the word of the Lord to Zerubbabel: 'Not by might nor by power, but by my Spirit,' says the Lord Almighty.*
>
> *7 "What are you, mighty mountain? Before Zerubbabel you will become level ground. Then he will bring out the capstone to shouts of 'God bless it! God bless it!'"*
>
> *Zechariah 4:6-7(NIV)*

You are Strong in Body

Being strong in body is about honoring God with your body. Being strong in body is about achieving and maintaining good health and setting an example for others, especially the next generation. God desires that you be physically fit so that you can enjoy life and function as you were uniquely designed to do. Despite whatever limitations (that are beyond your control) you may have, God has called you to work. You have a God-given assignment, and hopefully have developed your *God why*. Just as God wants you to be strong in mind and spirit, He wants you to be strong in body. You are divinely designed for your unique destiny and your body is the key component to living out your purpose.

Before beginning any detox, you should check in with your healthcare provider to ensure that it is safe for you. I am not a proponent of the many popular detoxes and cleanses because I believe some do more harm than good to your body. However, one physical detox that I do recommend is a two week "sugar detox". This type of detox is beneficial because sugar is addictive and cutting out simple carbohydrates can be difficult; this detox often serves as a good jump start for any eating plan. On my brand of detox, you'll eat lean meat, fish, eggs, vegetables, and raw fruit—that's it. No juicing, no smoothies, no dairy, no processed foods, et cetera. Although many similar detoxes do not, I allow for consumption of raw fruit on my plan. Moreover, I actually encourage it. You'll have hard enough time cutting foods, and fruit can help take the edge off sugar withdrawals. After all, a detox should serve as a launch pad into a new lifestyle not as a punishment. This new lifestyle will promote longevity, good mental and spiritual health, along with a strong able body. It is a lifestyle that includes good (minimally processed) foods, regular aerobic exercise, and strength training.

Now Move!

It is time for action! You have all the information that you need to get started. You also have your *God why,* and you should begin to write your plan. Start with the sugar detox and, if you're new to exercise, add exercise in the second week of your detox. Be sure to write your plan all out and place it where you see it daily. You can make your plan in the form of an "I can list" or a traditional list, in the form of a calendar, or even in the form of a vision board. Do what speaks to you. Write it, make it plain and run with it!

Then the Lord answered me and said,

"Write the vision

And engrave it plainly on [clay] tablets

So that the one who reads it will run

Habakkuk 2:2 (AMP)

Once you have reached your health goal, maintaining it becomes key. Along with continuing to be mindful about water and sleep, you will still need to create the proper energy balance; most women need about 2,000 calories a day, and men about 2,500 calories a day for maintenance. Additionally, continue to do both cardio and resistance training. Continue to get better and stronger every year. Continue to honor God with your body.

Finally

Create a life that you love to live. Part of that will require creating communities around you that are conducive to the lifestyle you choose. Your communities influence who you are and who you will become in every aspect of life. Spending time with other believers will compel us to draw closer to God. Spending time with other professionals will compel you to drive harder in your career. Spending time with people who work out, and care for their bodies will compel you to try harder to care for your own. Spending time with people who are fiscally responsible will compel you to be a bit more mindful of your spending. Likewise, spending time with people who eat out often will likely result in you eating out more. See the trend yet? Believers need several communities; the community closest to you must be a community of believers who will continue to spur you on in the way of God. You likely have a professional community that you work with, as well as local community that you live in. Don't fall into the trap of thinking that, as a believer, your only community can be other believers. No, you, as we all are, are placed to effect change in each of your communities. To continuously cause change in your communities, you must continuously change yourself. You should always be striving to grow stronger. Continue to cultivate a strong mind, a strong spirit, and a strong body. This is the way to live the best life— one that benefits you, blesses others and gives God great Glory!